Cynthia's Revels

Ben Johnson

Contents

INTRODUCTION 7
CYNTHIA'S REVELS: 35
ACT I 46
ACT II 66
ACT III 84
ACT IV 101
ACT V 138

CYNTHIA'S REVELS

BY
Ben Johnson

INTRODUCTION

THE greatest of English dramatists except Shakespeare, the first literary dictator and poet-laureate, a writer of verse, prose, satire, and criticism who most potently of all the men of his time affected the subsequent course of English letters: such was Ben Jonson, and as such his strong personality assumes an interest to us almost unparalleled, at least in his age.

Ben Jonson came of the stock that was centuries after to give to the world Thomas Carlyle; for Jonson's grandfather was of Annandale, over the Solway, whence he migrated to England. Jonson's father lost his estate under Queen Mary, "having been cast into prison and forfeited." He entered the church, but died a month before his illustrious son was born, leaving his widow and child in poverty. Jonson's birthplace was Westminster, and the time of his birth early in 1573. He was thus nearly ten years Shakespeare's junior, and less well off, if a trifle better born. But Jonson did not profit even by this slight advantage. His mother married beneath her, a wright or bricklayer, and Jonson was for a time apprenticed to the trade. As a youth he attracted the attention of the famous antiquary, William Camden, then usher at Westminster School, and there the poet laid the solid foundations of his classical learning. Jonson always held Camden in veneration, acknowledging that to him he owed,

"All that I am in arts, all that I know;"

and dedicating his first dramatic success, "Every Man in His Humour," to him. It is doubtful whether Jonson ever went to either university, though Fuller says that he was "statutably admitted into St. John's College, Cambridge." He tells us that he took no degree, but was later "Master of Arts in both the universities, by their favour, not his study." When a mere youth Jonson enlisted as a soldier, trailing his pike in Flanders in the protracted wars of William the Silent against the Spanish. Jonson was a large and raw-boned lad; he became by his own account in time exceedingly bulky. In chat with his friend William Drummond of Hawthornden, Jonson told how "in his service in the Low Countries he had, in the face of both the camps, killed an enemy, and taken opima spolia from him;" and how "since his coming to England, being appealed to the fields, he had killed his adversary which had hurt him in the arm and whose sword was ten inches longer than his." Jonson's reach may have made up for the lack of his sword; certainly his prowess lost nothing in the telling. Obviously Jonson was brave, combative, and not averse to talking of himself and his doings.

In 1592, Jonson returned from abroad penniless. Soon after he married, almost as early and quite as imprudently as Shakespeare. He told Drummond curtly that "his wife was a shrew, yet honest"; for some years he lived apart from her in the household of Lord Albany. Yet two touching epitaphs among Jonson's "Epigrams," "On my first daughter," and "On my first son," attest the warmth of the poet's family affections. The daughter died in infancy, the son of the plague; another son grew up to manhood little credit to his father whom he survived. We know nothing beyond this of Jonson's domestic life.

How soon Jonson drifted into what we now call grandly "the theatrical profession" we do not know. In 1593, Marlowe made his tragic exit from life, and Greene, Shakespeare's other rival on the popular stage, had preceded Marlowe in an equally miserable death the year before. Shakespeare already had the running to himself. Jonson appears first in the employment of Philip Henslowe, the exploiter of several troupes of players, manager, and father-in-law of the famous actor, Edward Alleyn. From entries in "Henslowe's Diary," a species of theatrical account book which has been handed down to us, we know that Jonson was connected with the Admiral's men; for he borrowed 4 pounds of Henslowe, July 28, 1597, paying back 3s. 9d. on the same day on account of his "share" (in what is not altogether clear); while later, on December 3, of the same year, Henslowe advanced 20s. to him "upon a book which he showed the plot unto the company which he promised to deliver unto the company at Christmas next." In the next August Jonson was in collaboration with Chettle and Porter in a play called "Hot Anger Soon Cold." All this points to an association with Henslowe of some duration, as no mere tyro would be thus paid in advance upon mere promise. From allusions in Dekker's play, "Satiromastix," it appears that Jonson, like Shakespeare, began life as an actor, and that he "ambled in a leather pitch by a play-wagon" taking at one time the part of Hieronimo in Kyd's famous play, "The Spanish Tragedy." By the beginning of 1598, Jonson, though still in needy circumstances, had begun to receive recognition. Francis Meres -- well known for his "Comparative Discourse of our English Poets with the Greek, Latin, and Italian Poets," printed in 1598, and for his mention therein of a dozen plays of Shakespeare by title -- accords to Ben Jonson a place as one of "our best in tragedy," a matter of some surprise, as no known tragedy of Jonson from so early a date has come down to us. That Jonson was at work on tragedy, however, is proved by the entries in Henslowe of at least three tragedies, now lost, in which he had a hand. These are "Page of Plymouth," "King Robert II. of Scotland," and "Richard Crookback." But all of these came later, on his return to Henslowe, and range from August

1599 to June 1602.

Returning to the autumn of 1598, an event now happened to sever for a time Jonson's relations with Henslowe. In a letter to Alleyn, dated September 26 of that year, Henslowe writes: "I have lost one of my company that hurteth me greatly; that is Gabriel [Spencer], for he is slain in Hogsden fields by the hands of Benjamin Jonson, bricklayer." The last word is perhaps Henslowe's thrust at Jonson in his displeasure rather than a designation of his actual continuance at his trade up to this time. It is fair to Jonson to remark however, that his adversary appears to have been a notorious fire-eater who had shortly before killed one Feeke in a similar squabble. Duelling was a frequent occurrence of the time among gentlemen and the nobility; it was an impudent breach of the peace on the part of a player. This duel is the one which Jonson described years after to Drummond, and for it Jonson was duly arraigned at Old Bailey, tried, and convicted. He was sent to prison and such goods and chattels as he had "were forfeited." It is a thought to give one pause that, but for the ancient law permitting convicted felons to plead, as it was called, the benefit of clergy, Jonson might have been hanged for this deed. The circumstance that the poet could read and write saved him; and he received only a brand of the letter "T," for Tyburn, on his left thumb. While in jail Jonson became a Roman Catholic; but he returned to the faith of the Church of England a dozen years later.

On his release, in disgrace with Henslowe and his former associates, Jonson offered his services as a playwright to Henslowe's rivals, the Lord Chamberlain's company, in which Shakespeare was a prominent shareholder. A tradition of long standing, though not susceptible of proof in a court of law, narrates that Jonson had submitted the manuscript of "Every Man in His Humour" to the Chamberlain's men and had received from the company a refusal; that Shakespeare called him back, read the play himself, and at once accepted it. Whether this story is true or not, certain it is that "Every Man in His Humour" was accepted by Shakespeare's company and acted for the first time in 1598, with Shakespeare taking a part. The evidence of this is contained in the list of actors prefixed to the comedy in the folio of Jonson's works, 1616. But it is a mistake to infer, because Shakespeare's name stands first in the list of actors and the elder Kno'well first in the dramatis personae, that Shakespeare took that particular part. The order of a list of Elizabethan players was generally that of their importance or priority as shareholders in the company and seldom if ever corresponded to the list of characters.

"Every Man in His Humour" was an immediate success, and with it Jonson's reputation as one of the leading dramatists of his time was established once and for all. This could have been by no means Jonson's earliest comedy, and we have just learned that he was already reputed one of "our best in tragedy." Indeed, one of Jonson's extant comedies, "The Case is Altered," but one never claimed by him or published as his, must certainly have preceded "Every Man in His Humour" on the stage. The former play may be described as a comedy modelled on the Latin plays of Plautus. (It combines, in fact, situations derived from the "Captivi" and the "Aulularia" of that dramatist). But the pretty story of the beggar-maiden, Rachel, and her suitors, Jonson found, not among the classics, but in the ideals of romantic love which Shakespeare had already popularised on the stage. Jonson never again produced so fresh and lovable a feminine personage as Rachel, although in other respects "The Case is Altered" is not a conspicuous play, and, save for the satirising of Antony Munday in the person of Antonio Balladino and Gabriel Harvey as well, is perhaps the least characteristic of the comedies of Jonson.

"Every Man in His Humour," probably first acted late in the summer of 1598 and at the Curtain, is commonly regarded as an epoch-making play; and this view is not unjustified. As to plot, it tells little more than how an intercepted letter enabled a father to follow his supposedly studious son to London, and there observe his life with the gallants of the time. The real quality of this comedy is in its personages and in the theory upon which they are conceived. Ben Jonson had theories about poetry and the drama, and he was neither chary in talking of them nor in experimenting with them in his plays. This makes Jonson, like Dryden in his time, and Wordsworth much later, an author to reckon with; particularly when we remember that many of Jonson's notions came for a time definitely to prevail and to modify the whole trend of English poetry. First of all Jonson was a classicist, that is, he believed in restraint and precedent in art in opposition to the prevalent ungoverned and irresponsible Renaissance spirit. Jonson believed that there was a professional way of doing things which might be reached by a study of the best examples, and he found these examples for the most part among the ancients. To confine our attention to the drama, Jonson objected to the amateurishness and haphazard nature of many contemporary plays, and set himself to do something different; and the first and most striking thing that he evolved was his conception and practice of the comedy of humours.

As Jonson has been much misrepresented in this matter, let us quote his own words as to "humour." A humour, according to Jonson, was a bias of disposition, a warp, so to speak, in character by which

"Some one peculiar quality
Doth so possess a man, that it doth draw
All his affects, his spirits, and his powers,
In their conflictions, all to run one way."

But continuing, Jonson is careful to add:

"But that a rook by wearing a pied feather,
The cable hat-band, or the three-piled ruff,
A yard of shoe-tie, or the Switzers knot
On his French garters, should affect a humour!
O, it is more than most ridiculous."

Jonson's comedy of humours, in a word, conceived of stage personages on the basis of a ruling trait or passion (a notable simplification of actual life be it observed in passing); and, placing these typified traits in juxtaposition in their conflict and contrast, struck the spark of comedy. Downright, as his name indicates, is "a plain squire"; Bobadill's humour is that of the braggart who is incidentally, and with delightfully comic effect, a coward; Brainworm's humour is the finding out of things to the end of fooling everybody: of course he is fooled in the end himself. But it was not Jonson's theories alone that made the success of "Every Man in His Humour." The play is admirably written and each character is vividly conceived, and with a firm touch based on observation of the men of the London of the day. Jonson was neither in this, his first great comedy (nor in any other play that he wrote), a supine classicist, urging that English drama return to a slavish adherence to classical conditions. He says as to the laws of the old comedy (meaning by "laws," such matters as the unities of time and place and the use of chorus): "I see not then, but we should enjoy the same licence, or free power to illustrate and heighten our invention as they [the ancients] did; and not be tied to those strict and regular forms which the niceness of a few, who are nothing but form, would thrust upon us." "Every Man in His Humour" is written in prose, a novel practice which Jonson had of his predecessor in comedy, John Lyly. Even the word "humour" seems to have been employed in the Jonsonian sense by Chapman before Jonson's use of it. Indeed, the comedy of humours itself is only a heightened variety of the comedy of manners which represents life, viewed at a satirical angle, and is the oldest and most persistent species of comedy in the language. None the less, Jonson's comedy merited its immediate success and marked out a definite course in which comedy long continued to run. To mention only Shakespeare's Falstaff and his rout, Bardolph, Pistol, Dame Quickly, and the rest, whether in "Henry IV." or in "The Merry Wives of Windsor," all are conceived in the spirit of humours. So are the captains, Welsh, Scotch, and Irish of "Henry V.," and Malvolio especially later; though Shakespeare never employed the method of humours for an important personage. It was not Jonson's fault that many of his successors did precisely the thing that he had reprobated, that is, degrade "the humour: into an oddity of speech, an eccentricity of manner, of dress, or cut of beard. There was an anonymous play called "Every Woman in Her Humour." Chapman wrote "A Humourous Day's Mirth," Day, "Humour Out of Breath," Fletcher later, "The Humourous Lieutenant," and Jonson, besides "Every Man Out of His Humour," returned to the title in closing the cycle of his comedies in "The Magnetic Lady or Humours Reconciled."

With the performance of "Every Man Out of His Humour" in 1599, by Shakespeare's company once more at the Globe, we turn a new page in Jonson's career. Despite his many real virtues, if there is one feature more than any other that distinguishes Jonson, it is his arrogance; and to this may be added his self-righteousness, especially under criticism or satire. "Every Man Out of His Humour" is the first of three "comical satires" which Jonson contributed to what Dekker called the poetomachia or war of the theatres as recent critics have named it. This play as a fabric of plot is a very slight affair; but as a satirical picture of the manners of the time, proceeding by means of vivid caricature, couched in witty and brilliant dialogue and sustained by that righteous indignation which must lie at the heart of all true satire -- as a realisation, in short, of the classical ideal of comedy -- there had been nothing like Jonson's comedy since the days of Aristophanes. "Every Man in His Humour," like the two plays that follow it, contains two kinds of attack, the critical or generally satiric, levelled at abuses and corruptions in the abstract; and the personal, in which specific application is made of all this in the lampooning of poets and others, Jonson's contemporaries. The method of personal attack by actual caricature of a person on the stage is almost as old as the drama. Aristophanes so lampooned Euripides in "The Acharnians" and Socrates in "The Clouds," to mention no other examples; and in English drama this kind of thing is alluded to again and again. What Jonson really did, was to raise the dramatic lampoon to an art, and make out of a casual burlesque and bit of mimicry a dramatic satire of literary pretensions and permanency. With the arrogant attitude mentioned above and his uncommon eloquence in scorn, vituperation, and invective, it is no wonder that Jonson soon involved himself in literary and even personal quarrels with his fellow-authors. The circumstances of the origin of this 'poetomachia' are far from clear, and those who have written on the topic, except of late, have not helped to make them clearer. The origin of the "war" has been referred to satirical references, apparently to Jonson, contained in "The Scourge of Villainy," a satire in regular form after the manner of the ancients by John Marston, a fellow playwright, subsequent friend and collaborator of Jonson's. On the other hand, epigrams of Jonson have been discovered (49, 68, and 100) variously charging "playwright" (reasonably identified with Marston) with scurrility, cowardice, and plagiarism; though the dates of the epigrams cannot be ascertained with certainty. Jonson's own statement of the matter to Drummond runs: "He had many quarrels with Marston, beat him, and took his pistol from him, wrote his "Poetaster" on him; the beginning[s] of them were that Marston represented him on the stage."*

[Note] *The best account of this whole subject is to be found in the edition of "Poetaster" and "Satiromastrix" by J. H. Penniman in "Belles Lettres Series" shortly to appear. See also his earlier work, "The War of the Theatres," 1892, and the excellent contributions to the subject by H. C. Hart in "Notes and Queries," and in his edition of Jonson, 1906.

Here at least we are on certain ground; and the principals of the quarrel are known. "Histriomastix," a play revised by Marston in 1598, has been regarded as the one in which Jonson was thus "represented on the stage"; although the personage in question, Chrisogonus, a poet, satirist, and translator, poor but proud, and contemptuous of the common herd, seems rather a complimentary portrait of Jonson than a caricature. As to the personages actually ridiculed in "Every Man Out of His Humour," Carlo Buffone was formerly thought certainly to be Marston, as he was described as "a public, scurrilous, and profane jester," and elsewhere as the grand scourge or second untruss [that is, satirist], of the time" (Joseph Hall being by his own boast the first, and Marston's work being entitled "The Scourge of Villainy"). Apparently we must now prefer for Carlo a notorious character named Charles Chester, of whom gossipy and inaccurate Aubrey relates that he was "a bold impertinent fellow...a perpetual talker and made a noise like a drum in a room. So one time at a tavern Sir Walter Raleigh beats him and seals up his mouth (that is his upper and nether beard) with hard wax. From him Ben Jonson takes his Carlo Buffone ['i.e.', jester] in "Every Man in His Humour" ['sic']." Is it conceivable that after all Jonson was ridiculing Marston, and that the point of the satire consisted in an intentional confusion of "the grand scourge or second untruss" with "the scurrilous and profane" Chester?

We have digressed into detail in this particular case to exemplify the difficulties of criticism in its attempts to identify the allusions in these forgotten quarrels. We are on sounder ground of fact in recording other manifestations of Jonson's enmity. In "The Case is Altered" there is clear ridicule in the character Antonio Balladino of Anthony Munday, pageant-poet of the city, translator of romances and playwright as well. In "Every Man in His Humour" there is certainly a caricature of Samuel Daniel, accepted poet of the court, sonneteer, and companion of men of fashion. These men held recognised positions to which Jonson felt his talents better entitled him; they were hence to him his natural enemies. It seems almost certain that he pursued both in the personages of his satire through "Every Man Out of His Humour," and "Cynthia's Revels," Daniel under the characters Fastidious Brisk and Hedon, Munday as Puntarvolo and Amorphus; but in these last we venture on quagmire once more. Jonson's literary rivalry of Daniel is traceable again and again, in the entertainments that welcomed King James on his way to London, in the masques at court, and in the pastoral drama. As to Jonson's personal ambitions with respect to these two men, it is notable that he became, not pageant-poet, but chronologer to the City of London; and that, on the accession of the new king, he came soon to triumph over Daniel as the accepted entertainer of royalty.

"Cynthia's Revels," the second "comical satire," was acted in 1600, and, as a play, is even more lengthy, elaborate, and impossible than "Every Man Out of His Humour." Here personal satire seems to have absorbed everything, and while much of the caricature is admirable, especially in the detail of witty and trenchantly satirical dialogue, the central idea of a fountain of self-love is not very well carried out, and the persons revert at times to abstractions, the action to allegory. It adds to our wonder that this difficult drama should have been acted by the Children of Queen Elizabeth's Chapel, among them Nathaniel Field with whom Jonson read Horace and Martial, and whom he taught later how to make plays. Another of these precocious little actors was Salathiel Pavy, who died before he was thirteen, already famed for taking the parts of old men. Him Jonson immortalised in one of the sweetest of his epitaphs. An interesting sidelight is this on the character of this redoubtable and rugged satirist, that he should thus have befriended and tenderly remembered these little theatrical waifs, some of whom (as we know) had been literally kidnapped to be pressed into the service of the theatre and whipped to the conning of their difficult parts. To the caricature of Daniel and Munday in "Cynthia's Revels" must be added Anaides (impudence), here assuredly Marston, and Asotus (the prodigal), interpreted as Lodge or, more perilously, Raleigh. Crites, like Asper-Macilente in "Every Man Out of His Humour," is Jonson's self-complaisant portrait of himself, the just, wholly admirable, and judicious scholar, holding his head high above the pack of the yelping curs of envy and detraction, but careless of their puny attacks on his perfections with only too mindful a neglect.

The third and last of the "comical satires" is "Poetaster," acted, once more, by the Children of the Chapel in 1601, and Jonson's only avowed contribution to the fray. According to the author's own account, this play was written in fifteen weeks on a report that his enemies had entrusted to Dekker the preparation of "Satiromastix, the Untrussing of the Humorous Poet," a dramatic attack upon himself. In this attempt to forestall his enemies Jonson succeeded, and "Poetaster" was an immediate and deserved success. While hardly more closely knit in structure than its earlier companion pieces, "Poetaster" is planned to lead up to the ludicrous final scene in which, after a device borrowed from the

"Lexiphanes" of Lucian, the offending poetaster, Marston-Crispinus, is made to throw up the difficult words with which he had overburdened his stomach as well as overlarded his vocabulary. In the end Crispinus with his fellow, Dekker-Demetrius, is bound over to keep the peace and never thenceforward "malign, traduce, or detract the person or writings of Quintus Horatius Flaccus [Jonson] or any other eminent man transcending you in merit." One of the most diverting personages in Jonson's comedy is Captain Tucca. "His peculiarity" has been well described by Ward as "a buoyant blackguardism which recovers itself instantaneously from the most complete exposure, and a picturesqueness of speech like that of a walking dictionary of slang."

It was this character, Captain Tucca, that Dekker hit upon in his reply, "Satiromastix," and he amplified him, turning his abusive vocabulary back upon Jonson and adding "an immodesty to his dialogue that did not enter into Jonson's conception." It has been held, altogether plausibly, that when Dekker was engaged professionally, so to speak, to write a dramatic reply to Jonson, he was at work on a species of chronicle history, dealing with the story of Walter Terill in the reign of William Rufus. This he hurriedly adapted to include the satirical characters suggested by "Poetaster," and fashioned to convey the satire of his reply. The absurdity of placing Horace in the court of a Norman king is the result. But Dekker's play is not without its palpable hits at the arrogance, the literary pride, and self-righteousness of Jonson-Horace, whose "ningle" or pal, the absurd Asinius Bubo, has recently been shown to figure forth, in all likelihood, Jonson's friend, the poet Drayton. Slight and hastily adapted as is "Satiromastix," especially in a comparison with the better wrought and more significant satire of "Poetaster," the town awarded the palm to Dekker, not to Jonson; and Jonson gave over in consequence his practice of "comical satire." Though Jonson was cited to appear before the Lord Chief Justice to answer certain charges to the effect that he had attacked lawyers and soldiers in "Poetaster," nothing came of this complaint. It may be suspected that much of this furious clatter and give-and-take was pure playing to the gallery. The town was agog with the strife, and on no less an authority than Shakespeare ("Hamlet," ii. 2), we learn that the children's company (acting the plays of Jonson) did "so berattle the common stages...that many, wearing rapiers, are afraid of goose-quills, and dare scarce come thither."

Several other plays have been thought to bear a greater or less part in the war of the theatres. Among them the most important is a college play, entitled "The Return from Parnassus," dating 1601-02. In it a much-quoted passage makes Burbage, as a character, declare: "Why here's our fellow Shakespeare puts them all down; aye and Ben Jonson, too. O that Ben Jonson is a pestilent fellow; he brought up Horace, giving the poets a pill, but our fellow Shakespeare hath given him a purge that made him bewray his credit." Was Shakespeare then concerned in this war of the stages? And what could have been the nature of this "purge"? Among several suggestions, "Troilus and Cressida" has been thought by some to be the play in which Shakespeare thus "put down" his friend, Jonson. A wiser interpretation finds the "purge" in "Satiromastix," which, though not written by Shakespeare, was staged by his company, and therefore with his approval and under his direction as one of the leaders of that company.

The last years of the reign of Elizabeth thus saw Jonson recognised as a dramatist second only to Shakespeare, and not second even to him as a dramatic satirist. But Jonson now turned his talents to new fields. Plays on subjects derived from classical story and myth had held the stage from the beginning of the drama, so that Shakespeare was making no new departure when he wrote his "Julius

Caesar" about 1600. Therefore when Jonson staged "Sejanus," three years later and with Shakespeare's company once more, he was only following in the elder dramatist's footsteps. But Jonson's idea of a play on classical history, on the one hand, and Shakespeare's and the elder popular dramatists, on the other, were very different. Heywood some years before had put five straggling plays on the stage in quick succession, all derived from stories in Ovid and dramatised with little taste or discrimination. Shakespeare had a finer conception of form, but even he was contented to take all his ancient history from North's translation of Plutarch and dramatise his subject without further inquiry. Jonson was a scholar and a classical antiquarian. He reprobated this slipshod amateurishness, and wrote his "Sejanus" like a scholar, reading Tacitus, Suetonius, and other authorities, to be certain of his facts, his setting, and his atmosphere, and somewhat pedantically noting his authorities in the margin when he came to print. "Sejanus" is a tragedy of genuine dramatic power in which is told with discriminating taste the story of the haughty favourite of Tiberius with his tragical overthrow. Our drama presents no truer nor more painstaking representation of ancient Roman life than may be found in Jonson's "Sejanus" and "Catiline his Conspiracy," which followed in 1611. A passage in the address of the former play to the reader, in which Jonson refers to a collaboration in an earlier version, has led to the surmise that Shakespeare may have been that "worthier pen." There is no evidence to determine the matter.

In 1605, we find Jonson in active collaboration with Chapman and Marston in the admirable comedy of London life entitled "Eastward Hoe." In the previous year, Marston had dedicated his "Malcontent," in terms of fervid admiration, to Jonson; so that the wounds of the war of the theatres must have been long since healed. Between Jonson and Chapman there was the kinship of similar scholarly ideals. The two continued friends throughout life.

"Eastward Hoe" achieved the extraordinary popularity represented in a demand for three issues in one year. But this was not due entirely to the merits of the play. In its earliest version a passage which an irritable courtier conceived to be derogatory to his nation, the Scots, sent both Chapman and Jonson to jail; but the matter was soon patched up, for by this time Jonson had influence at court.

With the accession of King James, Jonson began his long and successful career as a writer of masques. He wrote more masques than all his competitors together, and they are of an extraordinary variety and poetic excellence. Jonson did not invent the masque; for such premeditated devices to set and frame, so to speak, a court ball had been known and practised in varying degrees of elaboration long before his time. But Jonson gave dramatic value to the masque, especially in his invention of the antimasque, a comedy or farcical element of relief, entrusted to professional players or dancers. He enhanced, as well, the beauty and dignity of those portions of the masque in which noble lords and ladies took their parts to create, by their gorgeous costumes and artistic grouping and evolutions, a sumptuous show. On the mechanical and scenic side Jonson had an inventive and ingenious partner in Inigo Jones, the royal architect, who more than any one man raised the standard of stage representation in the England of his day. Jonson continued active in the service of the court in the writing of masques and other entertainments far into the reign of King Charles; but, towards the end, a quarrel with Jones embittered his life, and the two testy old men appear to have become not only a constant irritation to each other, but intolerable bores at court. In "Hymenaei," "The Masque of Queens," "Love Freed from Ignorance," "Lovers made Men," "Pleasure Reconciled to Virtue," and many more will be found Jonson's aptitude, his taste, his poetry and inventiveness in these by-forms of the drama; while in "The Masque of Christmas," and "The Gipsies Metamorphosed" especially, is discoverable that power of broad comedy which, at court as well as in the city, was not the least element of Jonson's contemporary popularity.

But Jonson had by no means given up the popular stage when he turned to the amusement of King James. In 1605 "Volpone" was produced, "The Silent Woman" in 1609, "The Alchemist" in the following year. These comedies, with "Bartholomew Fair," 1614, represent Jonson at his height, and for constructive cleverness, character successfully conceived in the manner of caricature, wit and brilliancy of dialogue, they stand alone in English drama. "Volpone, or the Fox," is, in a sense, a transition play from the dramatic satires of the war of the theatres to the purer comedy represented in the plays named above. Its subject is a struggle of wit applied to chicanery; for among its dramatis personae, from the villainous Fox himself, his rascally servant Mosca, Voltore (the vulture), Corbaccio and Corvino (the big and the little raven), to Sir Politic Would-be and the rest, there is scarcely a virtuous character in the play. Question has been raised as to whether a story so forbidding can be considered a comedy, for, although the plot ends in the discomfiture and imprisonment of the most vicious, it involves no mortal catastrophe. But Jonson was on sound historical ground, for "Volpone" is conceived far more logically on the lines of the ancients' theory of comedy than was ever the romantic drama of Shakespeare, however repulsive we may find a philosophy of life that facilely divides the world into the rogues and their dupes, and, identifying brains with roguery and innocence with folly, admires the former while inconsistently punishing them.

"The Silent Woman" is a gigantic farce of the most ingenious construction. The whole comedy hinges on a huge joke, played by a heartless nephew on his misanthropic uncle, who is induced to take to himself a wife, young, fair, and warranted silent, but who, in the end, turns out neither silent nor a woman at all. In "The Alchemist," again, we have the utmost cleverness in construction, the whole fabric building climax on climax, witty, ingenious, and so plausibly presented that we forget its departures from the possibilities of life. In "The Alchemist" Jonson represented, none the less to the life, certain sharpers of the metropolis, revelling in their shrewdness and rascality and in the variety of the stupidity and wickedness of their victims. We may object to the fact that the only person in the play possessed of a scruple of honesty is discomfited, and that the greatest scoundrel of all is approved in the end and rewarded. The comedy is so admirably written and contrived, the personages stand out with such lifelike distinctness in their several kinds, and the whole is animated with such verve and resourcefulness that "The Alchemist" is a new marvel every time it is read. Lastly of this group comes the tremendous comedy, "Bartholomew Fair," less clear cut, less definite, and less structurally worthy of praise than its three predecessors, but full of the keenest and cleverest of satire and inventive to a degree beyond any English comedy save some other of Jonson's own. It is in "Bartholomew Fair" that we are presented to the immortal caricature of the Puritan, Zeal-in-the-Land Busy, and the Littlewits that group about him, and it is in this extraordinary comedy that the humour of Jonson, always open to this danger, loosens into the Rabelaisian mode that so delighted King James in "The Gipsies Metamorphosed." Another comedy of less merit is "The Devil is an Ass," acted in 1616. It was the failure of this play that caused Jonson to give over writing for the public stage for a period of nearly ten years.

"Volpone" was laid as to scene in Venice. Whether because of the success of "Eastward Hoe" or for other reasons, the other three comedies declare in the words of the prologue to "The Alchemist":

"Our scene is London, 'cause we would make known
No country's mirth is better than our own."

Indeed Jonson went further when he came to revise his plays for collected publication in his folio of 1616, he transferred the scene of "Every Man in His Humour" from Florence to London also, converting Signior Lorenzo di Pazzi to Old Kno'well, Prospero to Master Welborn, and Hesperida to Dame Kitely "dwelling i' the Old Jewry."

In his comedies of London life, despite his trend towards caricature, Jonson has shown himself a genuine realist, drawing from the life about him with an experience and insight rare in any generation. A happy comparison has been suggested between Ben Jonson and Charles Dickens. Both were men of the people, lowly born and hardly bred. Each knew the London of his time as few men knew it; and each represented it intimately and in elaborate detail. Both men were at heart moralists, seeking the truth by the exaggerated methods of humour and caricature; perverse, even wrong-headed at times, but possessed of a true pathos and largeness of heart, and when all has been said -- though the Elizabethan ran to satire, the Victorian to sentimentality -- leaving the world better for the art that they practised in it.

In 1616, the year of the death of Shakespeare, Jonson collected his plays, his poetry, and his masques for publication in a collective edition. This was an unusual thing at the time and had been attempted by no dramatist before Jonson. This volume published, in a carefully revised text, all the plays thus far mentioned, excepting "The Case is Altered," which Jonson did not acknowledge, "Bartholomew Fair," and "The Devil is an Ass," which was written too late. It included likewise a book of some hundred and thirty odd "Epigrams," in which form of brief and pungent writing Jonson was an acknowledged master; "The Forest," a smaller collection of lyric and occasional verse and some ten "Masques" and "Entertainments." In this same year Jonson was made poet laureate with a pension of one hundred marks a year. This, with his fees and returns from several noblemen, and the small earnings of his plays must have formed the bulk of his income. The poet appears to have done certain literary hack-work for others, as, for example, parts of the Punic Wars contributed to Raleigh's "History of the World." We know from a story, little to the credit of either, that Jonson accompanied Raleigh's son abroad in the capacity of a tutor. In 1618 Jonson was granted the reversion of the office of Master of the Revels, a post for which he was peculiarly fitted; but he did not live to enjoy its perquisites. Jonson was honoured with degrees by both universities, though when and under what circumstances is not known. It has been said that he narrowly escaped the honour of knighthood, which the satirists of the day averred King James was wont to lavish with an indiscriminate hand. Worse men were made knights in his day than worthy Ben Jonson.

From 1616 to the close of the reign of King James, Jonson produced nothing for the stage. But he "prosecuted" what he calls "his wonted studies" with such assiduity that he became in reality, as by report, one of the most learned men of his time. Jonson's theory of authorship involved a wide acquaintance with books and "an ability," as he put it, "to convert the substance or riches of another poet to his own use." Accordingly Jonson read not only the Greek and Latin classics down to the lesser writers, but he acquainted himself especially with the Latin writings of his learned contemporaries, their prose as well as their poetry, their antiquities and curious lore as well as their more solid learning. Though a poor man, Jonson was an indefatigable collector of books.

He told Drummond that "the Earl of Pembroke sent him 20 pounds every first day of the new year to buy new books." Unhappily, in 1623, his library was destroyed by fire, an accident serio-comically described in his witty poem, "An Execration upon Vulcan." Yet even now a book turns up from time to time in which is inscribed, in fair large Italian lettering, the name, Ben Jonson. With respect to Jonson's use of his material, Dryden said memorably of him: "[He] was not only a professed imitator of Horace, but a learned plagiary of all the others; you track him everywhere in their snow....But he has done his robberies so openly that one sees he fears not to be taxed by any law. He invades authors like a monarch, and what would be theft in other poets is only victory in him." And yet it is but fair to say that Jonson prided himself, and justly, on his originality. In "Catiline," he not only uses Sallust's account of the conspiracy, but he models some of the speeches of Cicero on the Roman orator's actual words. In "Poetaster," he lifts a whole satire out of Horace and dramatises it effectively for his purposes. The sophist Libanius suggests the situation of "The Silent Woman"; a Latin comedy of Giordano Bruno, "Il Candelaio," the relation of the dupes and the sharpers in "The Alchemist," the "Mostellaria" of Plautus, its admirable opening scene. But Jonson commonly bettered his sources, and putting the stamp of his sovereignty on whatever bullion he borrowed made it thenceforward to all time current and his own.

The lyric and especially the occasional poetry of Jonson has a peculiar merit. His theory demanded design and the perfection of literary finish. He was furthest from the rhapsodist and the careless singer of an idle day; and he believed that Apollo could only be worthily served in singing robes and laurel crowned. And yet many of Jonson's lyrics will live as long as the language. Who does not know "Queen and huntress, chaste and fair." "Drink to me only with thine eyes," or "Still to be neat, still to be dressed"?

Beautiful in form, deft and graceful in expression, with not a word too much or one that bears not its part in the total effect, there is yet about the lyrics of Jonson a certain stiffness and formality, a suspicion that they were not quite spontaneous and unbidden, but that they were carved, so to speak, with disproportionate labour by a potent man of letters whose habitual thought is on greater things. It is for these reasons that Jonson is even better in the epigram and in occasional verse where rhetorical finish and pointed wit less interfere with the spontaneity and emotion which we usually associate with lyrical poetry. There are no such epitaphs as Ben Jonson's, witness the charming ones on his own children, on Salathiel Pavy, the child-actor, and many more; and this even though the rigid law of mine and thine must now restore to William Browne of Tavistock the famous lines beginning: "Underneath this sable hearse." Jonson is unsurpassed, too, in the difficult poetry of compliment, seldom falling into fulsome praise and disproportionate similitude, yet showing again and again a generous appreciation of worth in others, a discriminating taste and a generous personal regard. There was no man in England of his rank so well known and universally beloved as Ben Jonson. The list of his friends, of those to whom he had written verses, and those who had written verses to him, includes the name of every man of prominence in the England of King James. And the tone of many of these productions discloses an affectionate familiarity that speaks for the amiable personality and sound worth of the laureate. In 1619, growing unwieldy through inactivity, Jonson hit upon the heroic remedy of a journey afoot to Scotland. On his way thither and back he was hospitably received at the houses of many friends and by those to whom his friends had recommended him. When he arrived in Edinburgh, the burgesses met to grant him the freedom of the city, and Drummond, foremost of Scottish poets, was proud to entertain him for weeks as his guest at Hawthornden. Some of the noblest of Jonson's poems were inspired by friendship. Such is the fine "Ode to the memory of Sir Lucius Cary and Sir Henry Moryson," and that admirable piece of critical insight and filial affection, prefixed to the first Shakespeare folio, "To the memory of my beloved master, William Shakespeare, and what he hath left us," to mention only these. Nor can the earlier "Epode," beginning "Not to know vice at all," be matched in stately gravity and gnomic wisdom in its own wise and stately age.

But if Jonson had deserted the stage after the publication of his folio and up to the end of the reign of King James, he was far from inactive; for year after year his inexhaustible inventiveness continued to contribute to the masquing and entertainment at court. In "The Golden Age Restored," Pallas turns the Iron Age with its attendant evils into statues which sink out of sight; in "Pleasure Reconciled to Virtue," Atlas figures represented as an old man, his shoulders covered with snow, and Comus, "the god of cheer or the belly," is one of the characters, a circumstance which an imaginative boy of ten, named John Milton, was not to forget. "Pan's Anniversary," late in the reign of James, proclaimed that Jonson had not yet forgotten how to write exquisite lyrics, and "The Gipsies Metamorphosed" displayed the old drollery and broad humorous stroke still unimpaired and unmatchable. These, too, and the earlier years of Charles were the days of the Apollo Room of the Devil Tavern where Jonson presided, the absolute monarch of English literary Bohemia. We hear of a room blazoned about with Jonson's own judicious "Leges Convivales" in letters of gold, of a company made up of the choicest spirits of the time, devotedly attached to their veteran dictator, his reminiscences, opinions, affections, and enmities. And we hear, too, of valorous potations; but in the words of Herrick addressed to his master, Jonson, at the Devil Tavern, as at the Dog, the Triple Tun, and at the Mermaid,

"We such clusters had
As made us nobly wild, not mad,
And yet each verse of thine
Outdid the meat, outdid the frolic wine."

But the patronage of the court failed in the days of King Charles, though Jonson was not without royal favours; and the old poet returned to the stage, producing, between 1625 and 1633, "The Staple of News," "The New Inn," "The Magnetic Lady," and "The Tale of a Tub," the last doubtless revised from a much earlier comedy. None of these plays met with any marked success, although the scathing generalisation of Dryden that designated them "Jonson's dotages" is unfair to their genuine merits. Thus the idea of an office for the gathering, proper dressing, and promulgation of news (wild flight of the fancy in its time) was an excellent subject for satire on the existing absurdities among newsmongers; although as much can hardly be said for "The Magnetic Lady," who, in her bounty, draws to her personages of differing humours to reconcile them in the end according to the alternative title, or "Humours Reconciled." These last plays of the old dramatist revert to caricature and the hard lines of allegory; the moralist is more than ever present, the satire degenerates into personal lampoon, especially of his sometime friend, Inigo Jones, who appears unworthily to have used his influence at court against the broken-down old poet. And now disease claimed Jonson, and he was bedridden for months. He had succeeded Middleton in 1628 as Chronologer to the City of London, but lost the post for not fulfilling its duties. King Charles befriended him, and even commissioned him to write still for the entertainment of the court; and he was not without the sustaining hand of noble patrons and devoted friends among the younger poets who were proud to be "sealed of the tribe of Ben."

Jonson died, August 6, 1637, and a second folio of his works, which he had been some time gathering, was printed in 1640, bearing in its various parts dates ranging from 1630 to 1642. It included all the plays mentioned in the foregoing paragraphs, excepting "The Case is Altered;" the masques, some fifteen, that date between 1617 and 1630; another collection of lyrics and occasional poetry called "Underwoods, including some further entertainments; a translation of "Horace's Art of Poetry" (also published in a vicesimo quarto in 1640), and certain fragments and ingatherings which the poet would hardly have included himself. These last comprise the fragment (less than seventy lines) of a tragedy called "Mortimer his Fall," and three acts of a pastoral drama of much beauty and poetic spirit, "The Sad Shepherd." There is also the exceedingly interesting "English Grammar" "made by Ben Jonson for the benefit of all strangers out of his observation of the English language now spoken and in use," in Latin and English; and "Timber, or Discoveries" "made upon men and matter as they have flowed out of his daily reading, or had their reflux to his peculiar notion of the times." The "Discoveries," as it is usually called, is a commonplace book such as many literary men have kept, in which their reading was chronicled, passages that took their fancy translated or transcribed, and their passing opinions noted. Many passages of Jonson's "Discoveries" are literal translations from the authors he chanced to be reading, with the reference, noted or not, as the accident of the moment prescribed. At times he follows the line of Macchiavelli's argument as to the nature and conduct of princes; at others he clarifies his own conception of poetry and poets by recourse to Aristotle. He finds a choice paragraph on eloquence in Seneca the elder and applies it to his own recollection of Bacon's power as an orator; and another on facile and ready genius, and translates it, adapting it to his recollection of his fellow-playwright, Shakespeare. To call such passages -- which Jonson never intended for publication --

plagiarism, is to obscure the significance of words. To disparage his memory by citing them is a preposterous use of scholarship. Jonson's prose, both in his dramas, in the descriptive comments of his masques, and in the "Discoveries," is characterised by clarity and vigorous directness, nor is it wanting in a fine sense of form or in the subtler graces of diction.

When Jonson died there was a project for a handsome monument to his memory. But the Civil War was at hand, and the project failed. A memorial, not insufficient, was carved on the stone covering his grave in one of the aisles of Westminster Abbey:

"O rare Ben Jonson."

FELIX E. SCHELLING.

THE COLLEGE,
PHILADELPHIA, U.S.A.

The following is a complete list of his published works: --

DRAMAS:
Every Man in his Humour, 4to, 1601;
The Case is Altered, 4to, 1609;
Every Man out of his Humour, 4to, 1600;
Cynthia's Revels, 4to, 1601;
Poetaster, 4to, 1602;
Sejanus, 4to, 1605;
Eastward Ho (with Chapman and Marston), 4to, 1605;
Volpone, 4to, 1607;
Epicoene, or the Silent Woman, 4to, 1609 (?), fol., 1616;
The Alchemist, 4to, 1612;
Catiline, his Conspiracy, 4to, 1611;

Bartholomew Fayre, 4to, 1614 (?), fol., 1631;
The Divell is an Asse, fol., 1631;
The Staple of Newes, fol., 1631;
The New Sun, 8vo, 1631, fol., 1692;
The Magnetic Lady, or Humours Reconcild, fol., 1640;
A Tale of a Tub, fol., 1640;
The Sad Shepherd, or a Tale of Robin Hood, fol., 1641;
Mortimer his Fall (fragment), fol., 1640.

To Jonson have also been attributed additions to Kyd's Jeronymo, and collaboration in The Widow with Fletcher and Middleton, and in the Bloody Brother with Fletcher.

POEMS:
Epigrams, The Forrest, Underwoods, published in fols., 1616, 1640;
Selections: Execration against Vulcan, and Epigrams, 1640;
G. Hor. Flaccus his art of Poetry, Englished by Ben Jonson, 1640;
Leges Convivialis, fol., 1692.
Other minor poems first appeared in Gifford's edition of Works.

PROSE:
Timber, or Discoveries made upon Men and Matter, fol., 1641;
The English Grammar, made by Ben Jonson for the benefit of Strangers, fol., 1640.

Masques and Entertainments were published in the early folios.

WORKS:
Fol., 1616, volume. 2, 1640 (1631-41);
fol., 1692, 1716-19, 1729;
edited by P. Whalley, 7 volumes., 1756;
by Gifford (with Memoir), 9 volumes., 1816, 1846;
re-edited by F. Cunningham, 3 volumes., 1871;

in 9 volumes., 1875;
by Barry Cornwall (with Memoir), 1838;
by B. Nicholson (Mermaid Series), with Introduction by
C. H. Herford, 1893, etc.;
Nine Plays, 1904;
ed. H. C. Hart (Standard Library), 1906, etc;
Plays and Poems, with Introduction by H. Morley (Universal
Library), 1885;
Plays (7) and Poems (Newnes), 1905;
Poems, with Memoir by H. Bennett (Carlton Classics), 1907;
Masques and Entertainments, ed. by H. Morley, 1890.

SELECTIONS:
J. A. Symonds, with Biographical and Critical Essay,
(Canterbury Poets), 1886;
Grosart, Brave Translunary Things, 1895;
Arber, Jonson Anthology, 1901;
Underwoods, Cambridge University Press, 1905;
Lyrics (Jonson, Beaumont and Fletcher), the Chap Books,
No. 4, 1906;
Songs (from Plays, Masques, etc.), with earliest known
setting, Eragny Press, 1906.

LIFE:
See Memoirs affixed to Works;
J. A. Symonds (English Worthies), 1886;
Notes of Ben Jonson Conversations with Drummond of Hawthornden;
Shakespeare Society, 1842;
ed. with Introduction and Notes by P. Sidney, 1906;
Swinburne, A Study of Ben Jonson, 1889.

***

CYNTHIA'S REVELS:

OR, THE FOUNTAIN OF SELF-LOVE

TO THE SPECIAL FOUNTAIN OF MANNERS

THE COURT

THOU art a bountiful and brave spring, and waterest all the noble plants of this island. In thee the whole kingdom dresseth itself, and is ambitious to use thee as her glass. Beware then thou render men's figures truly, and teach them no less to hate their deformities, than to love their forms: for, to grace, there should come reverence; and no man can call that lovely, which is not also venerable. It is not powdering, perfuming, and every day smelling of the tailor, that converteth to a beautiful object: but a mind shining through any suit, which needs no false light, either of riches or honours, to help it. Such shalt thou find some here, even in the reign of Cynthia, -- a Crites and an Arete. Now, under thy Phoebus, it will be thy province to make more; except thou desirest to have thy source mix with the spring of self-love, and so wilt draw upon thee as welcome a discovery of thy days, as was then made of her nights.

Thy servant, but not slave,
BEN JONSON.

DRAMATIS PERSONAE.

CYNTHIA.
ECHO.
MERCURY.
ARETE.
HESPERUS.
PHANTASTE.
CRITES.
ARGURION.
AMORPHUS.
PHILAUTIA.
ASOTUS.
MORIA.
HEDON.
COS.
ANAIDES.
GELAIA.
MORPHIDES.
PROSAITES.
MORUS.
CUPID.

MUTES. -- PHRONESIS, THAUMA, TIME

SCENE, -- GARGAPHIE

INDUCTION.

THE STAGE.

AFTER THE SECOND SOUNDING.

ENTER THREE OF THE CHILDREN, STRUGGLING.

1 CHILD. Pray you away; why, fellows! Gods so, what do you mean?

2 CHILD. Marry, that you shall not speak the prologue sir.

3 CHILD. Why, do you hope to speak it?

2 CHILD. Ay, and I think I have most right to it: I am sure I studied it first.

3 CHILD. That's all one, if the author think I can speak it better.

1 CHILD. I plead possession of the cloak: gentles, your suffrages, I pray you.

[WITHIN.] Why children! are you not ashamed? come in there.

3 CHILD. Slid, I'll play nothing in the play: unless I speak it.

1 CHILD. Why, will you stand to most voices of the gentlemen? let that decide it.

3 CHILD. O, no, sir gallant; you presume to have the start of us there, and that makes you offer so prodigally.

1 CHILD. No, would I were whipped if I had any such thought; try it by lots either.

2 CHILD. Faith, I dare tempt my fortune in a greater venture than this.

3 CHILD. Well said, resolute Jack! I am content too; so we draw first. Make the cuts.

1 CHILD. But will you not snatch my cloak while I am stooping?

3 CHILD. No, we scorn treachery.

2 CHILD. Which cut shall speak it?

3 CHILD. The shortest.

1 CHILD. Agreed: draw. [THEY DRAW CUTS.] The shortest is come to the shortest. Fortune was not altogether blind in this. Now, sir, I hope I shall go forward without your envy.

2 CHILD. A spite of all mischievous luck! I was once plucking at the other.

3 CHILD. Stay Jack: 'slid I'll do somewhat now afore I go in, though it be nothing but to revenge myself on the author; since I

speak not his prologue, I'll go tell all the argument of his play afore-hand, and so stale his invention to the auditory, before it come forth.

1 CHILD. O, do not so.

2 CHILD. By no means.

3 CHILD. [ADVANCING TO THE FRONT OF THE STAGE.] First, the title of his play is "Cynthia's Revels," as any man that hath hope to be saved by his book can witness; the scene, Gargaphie, which I do vehemently suspect for some fustian country; but let that vanish. Here is the court of Cynthia whither he brings Cupid travelling on foot, resolved to turn page. By the way Cupid meets with Mercury, (as that's a thing to be noted); take any of our play-books without a Cupid or a Mercury in it, and burn it for an heretic in poetry. -- [IN THESE AND THE SUBSEQUENT SPEECHES, AT EVERY BREAK, THE OTHER
TWO INTERRUPT, AND ENDEAVOUR TO STOP HIM.] Pray thee, let me alone. Mercury, he in the nature of a conjurer, raises up Echo, who weeps over her love, or daffodil, Narcissus, a little; sings; curses the spring wherein the pretty foolish gentleman melted himself away: and there's an end of her. -- Now I am to inform you, that Cupid and Mercury do both become pages. Cupid attends on Philautia, or Self-love, a court lady: Mercury follows Hedon, the Voluptuous, and a courtier; one that ranks himself even with Anaides, or the Impudent, a gallant, and, that's my part; one that keeps Laughter, Gelaia, the daughter of Folly, a wench in boy's attire, to wait on him -- These, in the court, meet with Amorphus, or the deformed, a traveller that hath drunk of the fountain, and there tells the wonders of the water. They presently dispatch away their pages with bottles to fetch of it, and themselves go to visit the ladies. But I should have told you -- Look, these emmets put

me out here -- that with this Amorphus, there comes along a citizen's heir, Asotus, or the Prodigal, who, in imitation of the traveller, who hath the Whetstone following him, entertains the Beggar, to be his attendant. -- Now, the nymphs who are mistresses to these gallants, are Philautia, Self-love; Phantaste, a light Wittiness; Argurion, Money; and their guardian, mother Moria; or mistress Folly.

1 CHILD. Pray thee, no more.

3 CHILD. There Cupid strikes Money in love with the Prodigal, makes her dote upon him, give him jewels, bracelets, carcanets, etc. All which he most ingeniously departs withal to be made known to the other ladies and gallants; and in the heat of this, increases his train with the Fool to follow him, as well as the Beggar -- By this time, your Beggar begins to wait close, who is returned with the rest of his fellow bottlemen. -- There they all drink, save Argurion, who is fallen into a sudden apoplexy --

1 CHILD. Stop his mouth.

3 CHILD. And then there's a retired scholar there, you would not wish a thing to be better contemn'd of a society of gallants, than it is; and he applies his service, good gentleman, to the Lady Arete, or Virtue, a poor nymph of Cynthia's train, that's scarce able to buy herself a gown; you shall see her play in a black robe anon: a creature, that, I assure you, is no less scorn'd than himself. Where am I now? at a stand!

2 CHILD. Come, leave at last, yet.

3 CHILD. O, the night is come ('twas somewhat dark, methought), and Cynthia intends to come forth; that helps it a little yet. All

the courtiers must provide for revels; they conclude upon a masque, the device of which is -- What, will you ravish me? -- that each of these Vices, being to appear before Cynthia, would seem other than indeed they are; and therefore assume the most neighbouring Virtues as their masking habit -- I'd cry a rape, but that you are children.

2 CHILD. Come, we'll have no more of this anticipation; to give them the inventory of their cates aforehand, were the discipline of a tavern, and not fitting this presence.

1 CHILD. Tut, this was but to shew us the happiness of his memory. I thought at first he would have plaid the ignorant critic with everything along as he had gone; I expected some such device.

3 CHILD. O, you shall see me do that rarely; lend me thy cloak.

1 CHILD. Soft sir, you'll speak my prologue in it.

3 CHILD. No, would I might never stir then.

2 CHILD. Lend it him, lend it him:

1 CHILD. Well, you have sworn. [GIVES HIM THE CLOAK.]

3 CHILD. I have. Now, sir; suppose I am one of your genteel auditors, that am come in, having paid my money at the door, with much ado, and here I take my place and sit down: I have my three sorts of tobacco in my pocket, my light by me, and thus I begin. [AT THE BREAKS HE TAKES HIS TOBACCO.] By this light, I wonder that any man is so mad, to come to see these rascally tits play here -- They do act like so many wrens or pismires -- not the fifth part of a good face amongst them all. -- And then their music is abominable

-- able to stretch a man's ears worse then ten -- pillories and their ditties -- most lamentable things, like the pitiful fellows that make them -- poets. By this vapour, an 'twere not for tobacco -- I think -- the very stench of 'em would poison me, I should not dare to come in at their gates -- A man were better visit fifteen jails -- or a dozen or two of hospitals -- than once adventure to come near them. How is't? well?

1 CHILD. Excellent; give me my cloak.

3 CHILD. Stay; you shall see me do another now: but a more sober, or better-gather'd gallant; that is, as it may be thought, some friend, or well-wisher to the house: and here I enter.

1 CHILD. What? upon the stage too?

2 CHILD. Yes; and I step forth like one of the children, and ask you. Would you have a stool sir?

3 CHILD. A stool, boy!

2 CHILD. Ay, sir, if you'll give me sixpence, I'll fetch you one.

3 CHILD. For what, I pray thee? what shall I do with it?

2 CHILD. O lord, sir! will you betray your ignorance so much? why throne yourself in state on the stage, as other gentlemen use, sir.

3 CHILD. Away, wag; what would'st thou make an implement of me? 'Slid, the boy takes me for a piece of perspective, I hold my life, or some silk curtain, come to hang the stage here! Sir crack, I am none of your fresh pictures, that use to beautify the decayed dead

arras in a public theatre.

2 CHILD. 'Tis a sign, sir, you put not that confidence in your good clothes, and your better face, that a gentleman should do, sir. But I pray you sir, let me be a suitor to you, that you will quit our stage then, and take a place; the play is instantly to begin.

3 CHILD. Most willingly, my good wag; but I would speak with your author: where is he?

2 CHILD. Not this way, I assure you sir; we are not so officiously befriended by him, as to have his presence in the tiring-house, to prompt us aloud, stamp at the book-holder, swear for our properties, curse the poor tireman, rail the music out of tune, and sweat for every venial trespass we commit, as some author would, if he had such fine enghles as we. Well, 'tis but our hard fortune!

3 CHILD. Nay, crack, be not disheartened.

2 CHILD. Not I sir; but if you please to confer with our author, by attorney, you may, sir; our proper self here, stands for him.

3 CHILD. Troth, I have no such serious affair to negotiate with him; but what may very safely be turn'd upon thy trust. It is in the general behalf of this fair society here that I am to speak; at least the more judicious part of it: which seems much distasted with the immodest and obscene writing of many in their plays. Besides, they could wish your poets would leave to be promoters of other men's jests, and to way-lay all the stale apothegms, or old books they can hear of, in print or otherwise, to farce their scenes withal. That they would not so penuriously glean wit from every laundress or hackney-man; or derive their best grace, with

servile imitation, from common stages, or observation of the company they converse with; as if their invention lived wholly upon another man's trencher. Again, that feeding their friends with nothing of their own, but what they have twice or thrice cooked, they should not wantonly give out, how soon they had drest it; nor how many coaches came to carry away the broken meat, besides hobby-horses and foot-cloth nags.

2 CHILD. So, sir, this is all the reformation you seek?

3 CHILD. It is; do not you think it necessary to be practised, my little wag?

2 CHILD. Yes, where any such ill-habited custom is received.

3 CHILD. O (I had almost forgot it too), they say, the umbrae, or ghosts of some three or four plays departed a dozen years since, have been seen walking on your stage here; take heed boy, if your house be haunted with such hobgoblins, 'twill fright away all your spectators quickly.

2 CHILD. Good, sir; but what will you say now, if a poet, untouch'd with any breath of this disease, find the tokens upon you, that are of the auditory? As some one civet-wit among you, that knows no other learning, than the price of satin and velvets: nor other perfection than the wearing of a neat suit; and yet will censure as desperately as the most profess'd critic in the house, presuming his clothes should bear him out in it. Another, whom it hath pleased nature to furnish with more beard than brain, prunes his mustaccio; lisps, and, with some score of affected oaths, swears down all that sit about him; "That the old Hieronimo, as it was first acted, was the only best, and judiciously penn'd play of Europe". A third great-bellied juggler talks of twenty years

since, and when Monsieur was here, and would enforce all wits to be
of that fashion, because his doublet is still so. A fourth
miscalls all by the name of fustian, that his grounded capacity
cannot aspire to. A fifth only shakes his bottle head, and out of
his corky brain squeezeth out a pitiful learned face, and is
silent.

3 CHILD. By my faith, Jack, you have put me down: I would I knew
how to get off with any indifferent grace! here take your cloak,
and promise some satisfaction in your prologue, or, I'll be sworn
we have marr'd all.

2 CHILD. Tut, fear not, child, this will never distaste a true
sense: be not out, and good enough. I would thou hadst some sugar
candied to sweeten thy mouth.

THE THIRD SOUNDING.

PROLOGUE.

If gracious silence, sweet attention,
Quick sight, and quicker apprehension,
The lights of judgment's throne, shine any where,
Our doubtful author hopes this is their sphere;
And therefore opens he himself to those,
To other weaker beams his labours close,
As loth to prostitute their virgin-strain,
To every vulgar and adulterate brain.
In this alone, his Muse her sweetness hath,
She shuns the print of any beaten path;
And proves new ways to come to learned ears:

Pied ignorance she neither loves, nor fears.
Nor hunts she after popular applause,
Or foamy praise, that drops from common jaws
The garland that she wears, their hands must twine,
Who can both censure, understand, define
What merit is: then cast those piercing rays,
Round as a crown, instead of honour'd bays,
About his poesy; which, he knows, affords
Words, above action; matter, above words.

ACT I

SCENE I. -- A GROVE AND FOUNTAIN.

ENTER CUPID, AND MERCURY WITH HIS CADUCEUS, ON DIFFERENT SIDES.

CUP. Who goes there?

MER. 'Tis I, blind archer.

CUP. Who, Mercury?

MER. Ay.

CUP. Farewell.

MER. Stay Cupid.

CUP. Not in your company, Hermes, except your hands were riveted at your back.

MER. Why so, my little rover?

CUP. Because I know you have not a finger, but is as long as my quiver, cousin Mercury, when you please to extend it.

MER. Whence derive you this speech, boy?

CUP. O! 'tis your best polity to be ignorant. You did never steal Mars his sword out of the sheath, you! nor Neptune's trident! nor Apollo's bow! no, not you! Alas, your palms, Jupiter knows, they are as tender as the foot of a foundered nag, or a lady's face new mercuried, they'll touch nothing.

MER. Go to, infant, you'll be daring still.

CUP. Daring! O Janus! what a word is there? why, my light feather-heel'd coz, what are you any more than my uncle Jove's pander? a lacquey that runs on errands for him, and can whisper a light message to a loose wench with some round volubility? wait mannerly at a table with a trencher, warble upon a crowd a little, and fill out nectar when Ganymede's away? one that sweeps the god's drinking-room every morning, and sets the cushions in order again, which they threw one at another's head over night; can brush the carpets, call the stools again to their places, play the crier of the court with an audible voice, and take state of a president upon you at wrestlings, pleadings, negociations, etc. Here's the catalogue of your employments, now! O, no, I err; you have the marshalling of all the ghosts too that pass the Stygian ferry, and I suspect you for a share with the old sculler there, if the truth were known; but let that scape. One other peculiar virtue you possess, in lifting, or leiger-du-main, which few of the house of heaven have else besides, I must confess. But, methinks, that should not make you put that extreme distance 'twixt yourself and others, that we should be said to "over-dare" in speaking to your nimble deity. So Hercules might challenge priority of us both, because he can throw the bar farther, or lift more join'd stools at the arm's end, than we. If this might carry it, then we, who have made the whole body of divinity tremble at the twang of our bow, and enforc'd Saturnius himself to lay by his curled front, thunder, and three-fork'd fires, and put on a masking suit, too light for a reveller of eighteen to be seen in --

MER. How now! my dancing braggart in decimo sexto! charm your skipping tongue, or I'll --

CUP. What! use the virtue of your snaky tip staff there upon us?

MER. No, boy, but the smart vigour of my palm about your ears. You have forgot since I took your heels up into air, on the very hour I was born, in sight of all the bench of deities, when the silver roof of the Olympian palace rung again with applause of the fact.

CUP. O no, I remember it freshly, and by a particular instance; for my mother Venus, at the same time, but stoop'd to embrace you, and, to speak by metaphor, you borrow'd a girdle of her's, as you did Jove's sceptre while he was laughing; and would have done his thunder too, but that 'twas too hot for your itching fingers.

MER. 'Tis well, sir.

CUP. I heard, you but look'd in at Vulcan's forge the other day, and entreated a pair of his new tongs along with you for company: 'tis joy on you, i' faith, that you will keep your hook'd talons in practice with any thing. 'Slight, now you are on earth, we shall have you filch spoons and candlesticks rather than fail: pray Jove the perfum'd courtiers keep their casting-bottles, pick-tooths, and shittle-cocks from you, or our more ordinary gallants their tobacco-boxes; for I am strangely jealous of your nails.

MER. Never trust me, Cupid, but you are turn'd a most acute gallant of late! the edge of my wit is clean taken off with the fine and subtile stroke of your thin-ground tongue; you fight with too poignant a phrase, for me to deal with.

CUP. O Hermes, your craft cannot make me confident. I know my own steel to be almost spent, and therefore entreat my peace with you, in time: you are too cunning for me to encounter at length, and I think it my safest ward to close.

MER. Well, for once, I'll suffer you to win upon me, wag; but use not these strains too often, they'll stretch my patience. Whither might you march, now?

CUP. Faith, to recover thy good thoughts, I'll discover my whole project. The huntress and queen of these groves, Diana, in regard of some black and envious slanders hourly breathed against her, for her divine justice on Acteon, as she pretends, hath here in the vale of Gargaphie, proclaim'd a solemn revels, which (her godhead put off) she will descend to grace, with the full and royal expense of one of her clearest moons: in which time it shall be lawful for all sorts of ingenious persons to visit her palace, to court her nymphs, to exercise all variety of generous and noble pastimes; as well to intimate how far she treads such malicious imputations beneath her, as also to shew how clear her beauties are from the least wrinkle of austerity they may be charged with.

MER. But, what is all this to Cupid?

CUP. Here do I mean to put off the title of a god, and take the habit of a page, in which disguise, during the interim of these revels, I will get to follow some one of Diana's maids, where, if my bow hold, and my shafts fly but with half the willingness and aim they are directed, I doubt not but I shall really redeem the minutes I have lost, by their so long and over nice proscription of my deity from their court.

MER. Pursue it, divine Cupid, it will be rare.

CUP. But will Hermes second me?

MER. I am now to put in act an especial designment from my father Jove; but, that perform'd, I am for any fresh action that offers itself.

CUP. Well, then we part. [EXIT.]

MER. Farewell good wag.
Now to my charge.--Echo, fair Echo speak,
'Tis Mercury that calls thee; sorrowful nymph,
Salute me with thy repercussive voice,
That I may know what cavern of the earth,
Contains thy airy spirit, how, or where
I may direct my speech, that thou may'st hear.

ECHO. [BELOW] Here.

MER. So nigh!

ECHO. Ay.

MER. Know, gentle soul, then, I am sent from Jove,

Who, pitying the sad burthen of thy woes,
Still growing on thee, in thy want of words
To vent thy passion for Narcissus' death,
Commands, that now, after three thousand years,
Which have been exercised in Juno's spite,
Thou take a corporal figure and ascend,
Enrich'd with vocal and articulate power.
Make haste, sad nymph, thrice shall my winged rod
Strike the obsequious earth, to give thee way.
Arise, and speak thy sorrows, Echo, rise,
Here, by this fountain, where thy love did pine,
Whose memory lives fresh to vulgar fame,
Shrined in this yellow flower, that bears his name.

ECHO. [ASCENDS.] His name revives, and lifts me up from earth,
O, which way shall I first convert myself,
Or in what mood shall I essay to speak,
That, in a moment, I may be deliver'd
Of the prodigious grief I go withal?
See, see, the mourning fount, whose springs weep yet
Th' untimely fate of that too beauteous boy,
That trophy of self-love, and spoil of nature,
Who, now transform'd into this drooping flower,
Hangs the repentant head, back from the stream,
As if it wish'd, "Would I had never look'd
In such a flattering mirror!" O Narcissus,
Thou that wast once, and yet art, my Narcissus,
Had Echo but been private with thy thoughts,
She would have dropt away herself in tears,
Till she had all turn'd water; that in her,
As in a truer glass, thou might'st have gazed
And seen thy beauties by more kind reflection,
But self-love never yet could look on truth

But with blear'd beams; slick flattery and she
Are twin-born sisters, and so mix their eyes,
As if you sever one, the other dies.
Why did the gods give thee a heavenly form,
And earthly thoughts to make thee proud of it?
Why do I ask? 'Tis now the known disease
That beauty hath, to bear too deep a sense
Of her own self-conceived excellence.
O, hadst thou known the worth of heaven's rich gift,
Thou wouldst have turn'd it to a truer use,
And not with starv'd and covetous ignorance,
Pined in continual eyeing that bright gem,
The glance whereof to others had been more,
Than to thy famish'd mind the wide world's store:
So wretched is it to be merely rich!
Witness thy youth's dear sweets here spent untasted,
Like a fair taper, with his own flame wasted.

MER. Echo be brief, Saturnia is abroad,
And if she hear, she'll storm at Jove's high will.

CUP. I will, kind Mercury, be brief as time.
Vouchsafe me, I may do him these last rites,
But kiss his flower, and sing some mourning strain
Over his wat'ry hearse.

MER. Thou dost obtain;
I were no son to Jove, should I deny thee,
Begin, and more to grace thy cunning voice,
The humorous air shall mix her solemn tunes
With thy sad words: strike, music from the spheres,
And with your golden raptures swell our ears.

ECHO. [ACCOMPANIED]

Slow, slow, fresh fount, keep time with my salt tears:
Yet, slower, yet; O faintly, gentle springs:
List to the heavy part the music bears,
Woe weeps out her division, when she sings.
Droop herbs and flowers,
Fall grief and showers;
Our beauties are not ours;
O, I could still,
Like melting snow upon some craggy hill,
Drop, drop, drop, drop,
Since nature's pride is now a wither'd daffodil. --

MER. Now have you done?

ECHO. Done presently, good Hermes: bide a little;
Suffer my thirsty eye to gaze awhile,
But e'en to taste the place, and I am vanish'd.

MER. Forego thy use and liberty of tongue,
And thou mayst dwell on earth, and sport thee there;

ECHO. Here young Acteon fell, pursued, and torn
By Cynthia's wrath, more eager than his hounds;
And here -- ah me, the place is fatal! -- see
The weeping Niobe, translated hither
From Phrygian mountains; and by Phoebe rear'd,
As the proud trophy of her sharp revenge.

MER. Nay but hear --

ECHO. But here, O here, the fountain of self-love,

In which Latona, and her careless nymphs,
Regardless of my sorrows, bathe themselves
In hourly pleasures.

MER. Stint thy babbling tongue!
Fond Echo, thou profan'st the grace is done thee.
So idle worldlings merely made of voice,
Censure the powers above them. Come away,
Jove calls thee hence; and his will brooks no stay.

ECHO. O, stay: I have but one poor thought to clothe
In airy garments, and then, faith, I go.
Henceforth, thou treacherous and murdering spring,
Be ever call'd the FOUNTAIN OF SELF-LOVE:
And with thy water let this curse remain,
As an inseparate plague, that who but taste
A drop thereof, may, with the instant touch,
Grow dotingly enamour'd on themselves.
Now, Hermes, I have finish'd.

MER. Then thy speech
Must here forsake thee, Echo, and thy voice,
As it was wont, rebound but the last words.
Farewell.

ECHO. [RETIRING.] Well.

MER. Now, Cupid, I am for you, and your mirth,
To make me light before I leave the earth.

ENTER AMORPHUS, HASTILY.

AMO. Dear spark of beauty, make not so fast away:

ECHO. Away.

MER. Stay, let me observe this portent yet.

AMO. I am neither your Minotaur, nor your Centaur, nor your satyr, nor your hyaena, nor your babion, but your mere traveller, believe me.

ECHO. Leave me.

MER. I guess'd it should be some travelling motion pursued Echo so.

AMO. Know you from whom you fly? or whence?

ECHO. Hence. [EXIT.]

AMO. This is somewhat above strange: A nymph of her feature and lineament, to be so preposterously rude! well, I will but cool myself at yon spring, and follow her.

MER. Nay, then, I am familiar with the issue: I will leave you too. [EXIT.]

AMOR. I am a rhinoceros, if I had thought a creature of her symmetry would have dared so improportionable and abrupt a digression. -- Liberal and divine fount, suffer my profane hand to take of thy bounties. [TAKES UP SOME OF THE WATER.] By the purity of my taste, here is most ambrosiac water; I will sup of it again. By thy favour, sweet fount. See, the water, a more running, subtile, and humorous nymph than she permits me to touch, and handle her. What should I infer? if my behaviours had been of a cheap or customary garb; my accent or phrase vulgar; my garments trite; my countenance illiterate, or unpractised in the encounter of a beautiful and brave attired piece; then I might, with some change of colour, have suspected my faculties: But, knowing myself an essence so sublimated and refined by travel; of so studied and well exercised a gesture; so alone in fashion, able to render the face of any statesman living; and to speak the mere extraction of language, one that hath now made the sixth return upon venture; and was your first that ever enrich'd his country with the true laws of the duello; whose optics have drunk the spirit of beauty in some eight score and eighteen prince's courts, where I have resided, and been there fortunate in the amours of three hundred and forty and five ladies, all nobly, if not princely descended; whose names I have in catalogue: To conclude, in all so happy, as even admiration herself doth seem to fasten her kisses upon me: -- certes, I do neither see, nor feel, nor taste, nor savour the least steam or fume of a reason, that should invite this foolish, fastidious nymph, so peevishly to abandon me. Well, let the memory of her fleet into air; my thoughts and I am for this other element, water.

ENTER CRITES AND ASOTUS.

CRI. What, the well dieted Amorphus become a water-drinker! I see he means not to write verses then.

ASO. No, Crites! why?

CRI. Because --
Nulla placere diu, nec vivere carmina possunt,
Quae scribuntur aquae potoribus.

AMO. What say you to your Helicon?

CRI. O, the Muses' well! that's ever excepted.

AMO. Sir, your Muses have no such water, I assure you; your nectar, or the juice of your nepenthe, is nothing to it; 'tis above your metheglin, believe it.

ASO. Metheglin; what's that, sir? may I be so audacious to demand?

AMO. A kind of Greek wine I have met with, sir, in my travels; it is the same that Demosthenes usually drunk, in the composure of all his exquisite and mellifluous orations.

CRI. That's to be argued, Amorphus, if we may credit Lucian, who, in his "Encomio Demosthenis," affirms, he never drunk but water in any of his compositions.

AMO. Lucian is absurd, he knew nothing: I will believe mine own travels before all the Lucians of Europe. He doth feed you with fittons, figments, and leasings.

CRI. Indeed, I think, next a traveller, he does prettily well.

AMO. I assure you it was wine, I have tasted it, and from the hand of an Italian antiquary, who derives it authentically from the duke of Ferrara's bottles. How name you the gentleman you are in rank there with, sir?

CRI. 'Tis Asotus, son to the late deceased Philargyrus, the citizen.

AMO. Was his father of any eminent place or means?

CRI. He was to have been praetor next year.

AMO. Ha! a pretty formal young gallant, in good sooth; pity he is not more genteelly propagated. Hark you, Crites, you may say to him what I am, if you please; though I affect not popularity, yet I would loth to stand out to any, whom you shall vouchsafe to call friend.

CRI. Sir, I fear I may do wrong to your sufficiencies in the reporting them, by forgetting or misplacing some one: yourself can best inform him of yourself sir; except you had some catalogue or list of your faculties ready drawn, which you would request me to show him for you, and him to take notice of.

AMO. This Crites is sour: [ASIDE.] -- I will think, sir.

CRI. Do so, sir. -- O heaven! that anything in the likeness of man should suffer these rack'd extremities, for the uttering of his sophisticate good parts. [ASIDE.]

ASO. Crites, I have a suit to you; but you must not deny me; pray you make this gentleman and I friends.

CRI. Friends! why, is there any difference between you?

ASO. No; I mean acquaintance, to know one another.

CRI. O, now I apprehend you; your phrase was without me before.

ASO. In good faith, he's a most excellent rare man, I warrant him.

CRI. 'Slight, they are mutually enamour'd by this time. [ASIDE.]

ASO. Will you, sweet Crites?

CRI. Yes, yes.

ASO. Nay, but when? you'll defer it now, and forget it.

CRI. Why, is it a thing of such present necessity, that it requires so violent a dispatch!

ASO. No, but would I might never stir, he's a most ravishing man! Good Crites, you shall endear me to you, in good faith; la!

CRI. Well, your longing shall be satisfied, sir.

ASO. And withal, you may tell him what my father was, and how well he left me, and that I am his heir.

CRI. Leave it to me, I'll forget none of your dear graces, I warrant you.

ASO. Nay, I know you can better marshal these affairs than I can -- O gods! I'd give all the world, if I had it, for abundance of such acquaintance.

CRI. What ridiculous circumstance might I devise now, to bestow this reciprocal brace of butterflies one upon another? [ASIDE.]

AMO. Since I trod on this side the Alps, I was not so frozen in my invention. Let me see: to accost him with some choice remnant of Spanish, or Italian! that would indifferently express my languages now: marry, then, if he shall fall out to be ignorant, it were both hard, and harsh. How else? step into some ragioni del stato, and so make my induction! that were above him too; and out of his element I fear. Feign to have seen him in Venice or Padua! or some face near his in similitude! 'tis too pointed and open. No, it must be a more quaint and collateral device, as -- stay: to frame some encomiastic speech upon this our metropolis, or the wise magistrates thereof, in which politic number, 'tis odds but his father fill'd up a room? descend into a particular admiration of their justice, for the due measuring of coals, burning of cans, and such like? as also their religion, in pulling down a superstitious cross, and advancing a Venus; or Priapus, in place of it? ha! 'twill do well. Or to talk of some hospital, whose walls record his father a benefactor? or of so many buckets bestow'd on his parish church in his lifetime, with his name at length, for want of arms, trickt upon them? any of these. Or to praise the cleanness of the street wherein he dwelt? or the provident painting of his posts, against he should have been praetor? or, leaving his parent, come to some special ornament about himself, as his rapier, or some other of his accountrements? I have it: thanks, gracious Minerva!

ASO. Would I had but once spoke to him, and then -- He comes to me!

AMO. 'Tis a most curious and neatly wrought band this same, as I have seen, sir.

ASO. O lord, sir.

AMO. You forgive the humour of mine eye, in observing it.

CRI. His eye waters after it, it seems. [ASIDE.]

ASO. O lord, sir! there needs no such apology I assure you.

CRI. I am anticipated; they'll make a solemn deed of gift of themselves, you shall see. [ASIDE.]

AMO. Your riband too does most gracefully in troth.

ASO. 'Tis the most genteel and received wear now, sir.

AMO. Believe me, sir, I speak it not to humour you -- I have not seen a young gentleman, generally, put on his clothes with more judgment.

ASO. O, 'tis your pleasure to say so, sir.

AMO. No, as I am virtuous, being altogether untravell'd, it strikes me into wonder.

ASO. I do purpose to travel, sir, at spring.

AMO. I think I shall affect you, sir. This last speech of yours hath begun to make you dear to me.

ASO. O lord, sir! I would there were any thing in me, sir, that might appear worthy the least worthiness of your worth, sir. I protest, sir, I should endeavour to shew it, sir, with more than common regard sir.

CRI. O, here's rare motley, sir. [ASIDE.]

AMO. Both your desert, and your endeavours are plentiful, suspect them not: but your sweet disposition to travel, I assure you, hath made you another myself in mine eye, and struck me enamour'd on your beauties.

ASO. I would I were the fairest lady of France for your sake, sir! and yet I would travel too.

AMO. O, you should digress from yourself else: for, believe it, your travel is your only thing that rectifies, or, as the Italian says, "vi rendi pronto all' attioni," makes you fit for action.

ASO. I think it be great charge though, sir.

AMO. Charge! why 'tis nothing for a gentleman that goes private, as yourself, or so; my intelligence shall quit my charge at all time. Good faith, this hat hath possest mine eye exceedingly; 'tis so pretty and fantastic: what! is it a beaver?

ASO. Ay, sir, I'll assure you 'tis a beaver, it cost me eight crowns but this morning.

AMO. After your French account?

ASO. Yes, sir.

CRI. And so near his head! beshrew me, dangerous. [ASIDE.]

AMO. A very pretty fashion, believe me, and a most novel kind of trim: your band is conceited too!

ASO. Sir, it is all at your service.

AMO. O, pardon me.

ASO. I beseech you, sir, if you please to wear it, you shall do me a most infinite grace.

CRI. 'Slight, will he be prais'd out of his clothes?

ASO. By heaven, sir, I do not offer it you after the Italian manner; I would you should conceive so of me.

AMO. Sir, I shall fear to appear rude in denying your courtesies, especially being invited by so proper a distinction: May I pray your name, sir?

ASO. My name is Asotus, sir.

AMO. I take your love, gentle Asotus, but let me win you to receive this, in exchange. -- [THEY EXCHANGE BEAVERS.]

CRI. Heart! they'll change doublets anon. [ASIDE.]

AMO. And, from this time esteem yourself in the first rank of those few whom I profess to love. What make you in company of this scholar here? I will bring you known to gallants, as Anaides of the ordinary, Hedon the courtier, and others, whose society shall render you graced and respected: this is a trivial fellow, too mean, too cheap, too coarse for you to converse with.

ASO. 'Slid, this is not worth a crown, and mine cost me eight but this morning.

CRI. I looked when he would repent him, he has begun to be sad a good while.

AMO. Sir, shall I say to you for that hat? Be not so sad, be not so sad: It is a relic I could not so easily have departed with, but as the hieroglyphic of my affection; you shall alter it to what form you please, it will take any block; I have received it varied

on record to the three thousandth time, and not so few: It hath
these virtues beside: your head shall not ache under it, nor your
brain leave you, without license; It will preserve your complexion
to eternity; for no beam of the sun, should you wear it under zona
torrida, hath power to approach it by two ells. It is proof
against thunder, and enchantment; and was given me by a great man
in Russia, as an especial prized present; and constantly affirm'd
to be the hat that accompanied the politic Ulysses in his tedious
and ten years' travels.

ASO. By Jove, I will not depart withal, whosoever would give me a
million.

ENTER COS AND PROSAITES.

COS. Save you sweet bloods! does any of you want a creature, or a
dependent?

CRI. Beshrew me, a fine blunt slave!

AMO. A page of good timber! it will now be my grace to entertain
him first, though I cashier him again in private. -- How art thou
call'd?

COS. Cos, sir, Cos.

CRI. Cos! how happily hath fortune furnish'd him with a whetstone?

AMO. I do entertain you, Cos; conceal your quality till we be
private; if your parts be worthy of me, I will countenance you; if
not, catechise you. -- Gentles, shall we go?

ASO. Stay, sir: I'll but entertain this other fellow, and then --

I have a great humour to taste of this water too, but I'll come
again alone for that -- mark the place. -- What's your name, youth?

PROS. Prosaites, sir.

ASO. Prosaites! a very fine name; Crites, is it not?

CRI. Yes, and a very ancient one, sir, the Beggar.

ASO. Follow me, good Prosaites; let's talk.

[EXEUNT ALL BUT CRITES.]

CRI. He will rank even with you, ere't be long.
If you hold on your course. O, vanity
How are thy painted beauties doted on,
By light and empty idiots! how pursued
With open, and extended appetite!
How they do sweat, and run themselves from breath,
Raised on their toes, to catch thy airy forms,
Still turning giddy, till they reel like drunkards,
That buy the merry madness of one hour
With the long irksomeness of following time!
O, how despised and base a thing is man,
If he not strive to erect his grovelling thoughts
Above the strain of flesh? but how more cheap,
When, ev'n his best and understanding part,
The crown and strength of all his faculties,
Floats, like a dead drown'd body, on the stream
Of vulgar humour, mixt with common'st dregs!
I suffer for their guilt now, and my soul,
Like one that looks on ill-affected eyes,
Is hurt with mere intention on their follies.

Why will I view them then, my sense might ask me?
Or is't a rarity, or some new object,
That strains my strict observance to this point?
O, would it were! therein I could afford
My spirit should draw a little near to theirs,
To gaze on novelties; so vice were one.
Tut, she is stale, rank, foul; and were it not
That those that woo her greet her with lock'd eyes,
In spight of all th' impostures, paintings, drugs,
Which her bawd, Custom, dawbs her cheeks withal,
She would betray her loath'd and leprous face,
And fright the enamour'd dotards from themselves:
But such is the perverseness of our nature,
That if we once but fancy levity,
How antic and ridiculous soe'er
It suit with us, yet will our muffled thought
Choose rather not to see it, than avoid it:
And if we can but banish our own sense,
We act our mimic tricks with that free license,
That lust, that pleasure, that security;
As if we practised in a paste-board case,
And no one saw the motion, but the motion.
Well, check thy passion, lest it grow too loud:
While fools are pitied, they wax fat, and proud.

ACT II

SCENE I. -- THE COURT.

ENTER CUPID AND MERCURY, DISGUISED AS PAGES.

CUP. Why, this was most unexpectedly followed, my divine delicate

Mercury, by the beard of Jove, thou art a precious deity.

MER. Nay, Cupid, leave to speak improperly; since we are turn'd cracks, let's study to be like cracks; practise their language, and behaviours, and not with a dead imitation: Act freely, carelessly, and capriciously, as if our veins ran with quicksilver, and not utter a phrase, but what shall come forth steep'd in the very brine of conceit, and sparkle like salt in fire.

CUP. That's not every one's happiness, Hermes: Though you can presume upon the easiness and dexterity of your wit, you shall give me leave to be a little jealous of mine; and not desperately to hazard it after your capering humour.

MER. Nay, then, Cupid, I think we must have you hood-wink'd again; for you are grown too provident since your eyes were at liberty.

CUP. Not so, Mercury, I am still blind Cupid to thee.

MER. And what to the lady nymph you serve?

CUP. Troth, page, boy, and sirrah: these are all my titles.

MER. Then thou hast not altered thy name with thy disguise?

CUP. O, no, that had been supererogation; you shall never hear your courtier call but by one of these three.

MER. Faith, then both our fortunes are the same.

CUP. Why, what parcel of man hast thou lighted on for a master?

MER. Such a one as, before I begin to decipher him, I dare not affirm to be any thing less than a courtier. So much he is during this open time of revels, and would be longer, but that his means are to leave him shortly after. His name is Hedon, a gallant wholly consecrated to his pleasures.

CUP. Hedon! he uses much to my lady's chamber, I think.

MER. How is she call'd, and then I can shew thee?

CUP. Madame Philautia.

MER. O ay, he affects her very particularly indeed. These are his graces. He doth (besides me) keep a barber and a monkey; he has a rich wrought waistcoat to entertain his visitants in, with a cap almost suitable. His curtains and bedding are thought to be his own; his bathing-tub is not suspected. He loves to have a fencer, a pedant, and a musician seen in his lodging a-mornings.

CUP. And not a poet?

MER. Fie no: himself is a rhymer, and that's thought better than a poet. He is not lightly within to his mercer, no, though he come when he takes physic, which is commonly after his play. He beats a tailor very well, but a stocking-seller admirably: and so consequently any one he owes money to, that dares not resist him. He never makes general invitement, but against the publishing of a new suit; marry, then you shall have more drawn to his lodging, than come to the launching of some three ships; especially if he be furnish'd with supplies for the retiring of his old wardrobe from pawn: if not, he does hire a stock of apparel, and some forty or fifty pound in gold, for that forenoon to shew. He is thought a very necessary perfume for the presence, and for that only cause welcome thither: six milliners' shops afford you not the like scent. He courts ladies with how many great horse he hath rid that morning, or how oft he hath done the whole, or half the pommado in a seven-night before: and sometime ventures so far upon the virtue of his pomander, that he dares tell 'em, how many shirts he has sweat at tennis that week; but wisely conceals so many dozen of balls he is on the score. Here he comes, that is all this.

ENTER HEDON, ANAIDES, AND GELAIA.

HED. Boy!

MER. Sir.

HED. Are any of the ladies in the presence?

MER. None yet, sir.

HED. Give me some gold, -- more.

ANA. Is that thy boy, Hedon?

HED. Ay, what think'st thou of him?

ANA. I'd geld him; I warrant he has the philosopher's stone.

HED. Well said, my good melancholy devil: sirrah, I have devised one or two of the prettiest oaths, this morning in my bed, as ever thou heard'st, to protest withal in the presence.

ANA. Prithee, let's hear them.

HED. Soft, thou'lt use them afore me.

ANA. No, d--mn me then -- I have more oaths than I know how to utter, by this air.

HED. Faith, one is, "By the tip of your ear, sweet lady." Is it not pretty, and genteel?

ANA. Yes, for the person 'tis applied to, a lady. It should be light, and --

HED. Nay, the other is better, exceeds it much: the invention is farther fet too. "By the white valley that lies between the alpine hills of your bosom, I protest. -- "

ANA. Well, you travell'd for that, Hedon.

MER. Ay, in a map, where his eyes were but blind guides to his understanding, it seems.

HED. And then I have a salutation will nick all, by this caper: hay!

ANA. How is that?

HED. You know I call madam Philautia, my Honour; and she calls me her Ambition. Now, when I meet her in the presence anon, I will come to her, and say, "Sweet Honour, I have hitherto contented my sense with the lilies of your hand; but now I will taste the roses of your lip"; and, withal, kiss her: to which she cannot but blushing answer, "Nay now you are too ambitious." And then do I reply: "I cannot be too Ambitious of Honour, sweet lady." Will't not be good? ha? ha?

ANA. O, assure your soul.

HED. By heaven, I think 'twill be excellent: and a very politic achievement of a kiss.

ANA. I have thought upon one for Moria of a sudden too, if it take.

HED. What is't, my dear Invention?

ANA. Marry, I will come to her, (and she always wears a muff, if you be remembered,) and I will tell her, "Madam your whole self cannot but be perfectly wise; for your hands have wit enough to keep themselves warm."

HED. Now, before Jove, admirable! [GELAIA LAUGHS.] Look, thy page takes it too. By Phoebus, my sweet facetious rascal, I could eat water-gruel with thee a month for this jest, my dear rogue.

ANA. O, Hercules 'tis your only dish; above all your potatoes or oyster-pies in the world.

HED. I have ruminated upon a most rare wish too, and the prophecy to it; but I'll have some friend to be the prophet; as thus: I do wish myself one of my mistress's cioppini. Another demands, Why would he be one of his mistress's cioppini? a third answers, Because he would make her higher: a fourth shall say, That will make her proud: and a fifth shall conclude, Then do I prophesy pride will have a fall; -- and he shall give it her.

ANA. I will be your prophet. Gods so, it will be most exquisite; thou art a fine inventious rogue, sirrah.

HED. Nay, and I have posies for rings, too, and riddles, that they dream not of.

ANA. Tut, they'll do that, when they come to sleep on them, time enough: But were thy devices never in the presence yet, Hedon?

HED. O, no, I disdain that.

ANA. 'Twere good we went afore then, and brought them acquainted with the room where they shall act, lest the strangeness of it put them out of countenance, when they should come forth.

[EXEUNT HEDON AND ANAIDES.]

CUP. Is that a courtier, too.

MER. Troth, no; he has two essential parts of the courtier, pride and ignorance; marry, the rest come somewhat after the ordinary gallant. 'Tis Impudence itself, Anaides; one that speaks all that comes in his cheeks, and will blush no more than a sackbut. He lightly occupies the jester's room at the table, and keeps laughter, Gelaia, a wench in page's attire, following him in place of a squire, whom he now and then tickles with some strange ridiculous stuff, utter'd as his land came to him, by chance. He will censure or discourse of any thing, but as absurdly as you would wish. His fashion is not to take knowledge of him that is beneath him in clothes. He never drinks below the salt. He does naturally admire his wit that wears gold lace, or tissue: stabs any man that speaks more contemptibly of the scholar than he. He is a great proficient in all the illiberal sciences, as cheating, drinking, swaggering, whoring, and such like: never kneels but to pledge healths, nor prays but for a pipe of pudding-tobacco. He will blaspheme in his shirt. The oaths which he vomits at one supper would maintain a town of garrison in good swearing a twelvemonth. One other genuine quality he has which crowns all these, and that is this: to a friend in want, he will not depart with the weight of a soldered groat, lest the world might censure him prodigal, or report him a gull: marry, to his cockatrice or punquetto, half a dozen taffata gowns or satin kirtles in a pair or two of months, why, they are nothing.

CUP. I commend him, he is one of my clients.

[THEY RETIRE TO THE BACK OF THE STAGE.]

ENTER AMORPHUS, ASOTUS, AND COS.

AMO. Come, sir. You are now within regard of the presence, and see, the privacy of this room how sweetly it offers itself to our retired intendments. -- Page, cast a vigilant and enquiring eye about, that we be not rudely surprised by the approach of some ruder stranger.

COS. I warrant you, sir. I'll tell you when the wolf enters, fear nothing.

MER. O what a mass of benefit shall we possess, in being the invisible spectators of this strange show now to be acted!

AMO. Plant yourself there, sir; and observe me. You shall now, as well be the ocular, as the ear-witness, how clearly I can refel that paradox, or rather pseudodox, of those, which hold the face to be the index of the mind, which, I assure you, is not so in any politic creature: for instance; I will now give you the particular and distinct face of every your most noted species of persons, as your merchant, your scholar, your soldier, your lawyer, courtier, etc., and each of these so truly, as you would swear, but that your eye shall see the variation of the lineament, it were my most proper and genuine aspect. First, for your merchant, or city-face, 'tis thus; a dull, plodding-face, still looking in a direct line, forward: there is no great matter in this face. Then have you your student's, or academic face; which is here an honest, simple, and methodical face; but somewhat more spread then the former. The third is your soldier's face, a menacing and astounding face, that looks broad and big: the grace of his face consisteth much in a beard. The anti-face to this, is your lawyer's face, a contracted, subtile, and intricate face, full of quirks and turnings, a labyrinthean face, now angularly, now circularly, every way aspected. Next is your statist's face, a serious, solemn, and supercilious face, full of formal and square gravity; the eye, for the most part, deeply and artificially shadow'd; there is great judgment required in the making of this face. But now, to come to your face of faces, or courtier's face; 'tis of three sorts, according to our subdivision of a courtier, elementary, practic, and theoric. Your courtier theoric, is he that hath arrived to his farthest, and doth now know the court rather by speculation than practice; and this is his face: a fastidious and oblique face; that looks as it went with a vice, and were screw'd thus. Your courtier practic, is he that is yet in his path, his course, his way, and hath not touch'd the punctilio or point of his hopes; his face is here: a most promising, open, smooth, and overflowing face, that seems as it would run and pour itself into you: somewhat a northerly face. Your courtier elementary, is one but newly enter'd, or as it were in the alphabet, or ut-re-mi-fa-sol-la of courtship. Note well this face, for it is this you must practise.

ASO. I'll practise them all, if you please, sir.

AMO. Ay, hereafter you may: and it will not be altogether an ungrateful study. For, let your soul be assured of this, in any rank or profession whatever, the more general or major part of opinion goes with the face and simply respects nothing else. Therefore, if that can be made exactly, curiously, exquisitely, thoroughly, it is enough: but for the present you shall only apply yourself to this face of the elementary courtier, a light, revelling, and protesting face, now blushing, now smiling, which you may help much with a wanton wagging of your head, thus, (a feather will teach you,) or with kissing your finger that hath the ruby, or playing with some string of your band, which is a most quaint kind of melancholy besides: or, if among ladies, laughing loud, and crying up your own wit, though perhaps borrow'd, it is not amiss. Where is your page? call for your casting-bottle, and place your mirror in your hat, as I told you; so! Come, look not pale, observe me, set your face, and enter.

MER. O, for some excellent painter, to have taken the copy of all these faces! [ASIDE.]

ASO. Prosaites!

AMO. Fie! I premonish you of that: in the court, boy, lacquey, or sirrah.

COS. Master, lupus in -- O, 'tis Prosaites.

ENTER PROSAITES.

ASO. Sirrah, prepare my casting-bottle; I think I must be enforced to purchase me another page; you see how at hand Cos waits here.

[EXEUNT AMORPHUS, ASOTUS, COS, AND PROSAITES.]

MER. So will he too in time.

CUP. What's he Mercury?

MER. A notable smelt. One that hath newly entertain'd the beggar to follow him, but cannot get him to wait near enough. 'Tis Asotus, the heir of Philargyrus; but first I'll give ye the other's character, which may make his the clearer. He that is with him is Amorphus, a traveller, one so made out of the mixture of shreds of forms, that himself is truly deform'd. He walks most commonly with a clove or pick-tooth in his mouth, he is the very mint of compliment, all his behaviours are printed, his face is another volume of essays, and his beard is an Aristarchus. He speaks all cream skimm'd, and more affected than a dozen waiting women. He is his own promoter in every place. The wife of the ordinary gives him his diet to maintain her table in discourse; which, indeed, is a mere tyranny over her other guests, for he will usurp all the talk: ten constables are not so tedious. He is no great shifter; once a year his apparel is ready to revolt. He doth use much to arbitrate quarrels, and fights himself, exceeding well, out at a window. He will lie cheaper than any beggar, and louder than most clocks; for which he is right properly accommodated to the Whetstone, his page. The other gallant is his zany, and doth most of these tricks after him; sweats to imitate him in every thing to a hair, except a beard, which is not yet extant. He doth learn to make strange sauces, to eat anchovies, maccaroni, bovoli, fagioli, and caviare, because he loves them; speaks as he speaks, looks, walks, goes so in clothes and fashion: is in all as if he were moulded of him. Marry, before they met, he had other very pretty sufficiencies, which yet he retains some light impression of; as frequenting a dancing school, and grievously torturing strangers with inquisition after his grace in his galliard. He buys a fresh acquaintance at any rate. His eyes and his raiment confer much together as he goes in the street. He treads nicely like the fellow that walks upon ropes, especially the first Sunday of his silk stockings; and when he is most neat and new, you shall strip him with commendations.

CUP. Here comes another. [CRITES PASSES OVER THE STAGE.]

MER. Ay, but one of another strain, Cupid; This fellow weighs somewhat.

CUP. His name, Hermes?

MER. Crites. A creature of a most perfect and divine temper: one, in whom the humours and elements are peaceably met, without emulation of precedency; he is neither too fantastically melancholy, too slowly phlegmatic, too lightly sanguine, or too rashly choleric; but in all so composed and ordered; as it is clear Nature went about some full work, she did more than make a man when she made him. His discourse is like his behaviour, uncommon, but not unpleasing; he is prodigal of neither. He strives rather to be that which men call judicious, than to be thought so; and is so truly learned, that he affects not to shew it. He will think and speak his thought both freely; but as distant from depraving another man's merit, as proclaiming his own. For his valour, 'tis such, that he dares as little to offer any injury, as receive one. In sum, he hath a most ingenuous and sweet spirit, a sharp and season'd wit, a straight judgment and a strong mind. Fortune could never break him, nor make him less. He counts it his pleasure to despise pleasures, and is more delighted with good deeds than goods. It is a competency to him that he can be virtuous. He doth neither covet nor fear; he hath too much reason to do either; and that commends all things to him.

CUP. Not better than Mercury commends him.

MER. O, Cupid, 'tis beyond my deity to give him his due praises: I could leave my place in heaven to live among mortals, so I were sure to be no other than he.

CUP. 'Slight, I believe he is your minion, you seem to be so ravish'd with him.

MER. He's one I would not have a wry thought darted against, willingly.

CUP. No, but a straight shaft in his bosom I'll promise him, if I am Cytherea's son.

MER. Shall we go, Cupid?

CUP. Stay, and see the ladies now: they'll come presently. I'll help to paint them.

MER. What lay colour upon colour! that affords but an ill blazon.

CUP. Here comes metal to help it, the lady Argurion.

[ARGURION PASSES OVER THE STAGE.]

MER. Money, money.

CUP. The same. A nymph of a most wandering and giddy disposition, humorous as the air, she'll run from gallant to gallant, as they sit at primero in the presence, most strangely, and seldom stays with any. She spreads as she goes. To-day you shall have her look as clear and fresh as the morning, and to-morrow as melancholic as midnight. She takes special pleasure in a close obscure lodging,

and for that cause visits the city so often, where she has many
secret true concealing favourites. When she comes abroad she's
more loose and scattering than dust, and will fly from place to
place, as she were wrapped with a whirlwind. Your young student,
for the most part, she affects not, only salutes him, and away: a
poet, nor a philosopher, she is hardly brought to take any notice
of; no, though he be some part of an alchemist. She loves a player
well, and a lawyer infinitely; but your fool above all. She can do
much in court for the obtaining of any suit whatsoever, no door
but flies open to her, her presence is above a charm. The worst in
her is want of keeping state, and too much descending into inferior
and base offices; she's for any coarse employment you will put upon
her, as to be your procurer, or pander.

MER. Peace, Cupid, here comes more work for you, another character
or two.

ENTER PHANTASTE, MORIA, AND PHILAUTIA.

PHA. Stay sweet Philautia; I'll but change my fan, and go
presently.

MOR. Now, in very good serious, ladies, I will have this order
revers'd, the presence must be better maintain'd from you: a
quarter past eleven, and ne'er a nymph in prospective! Beshrew my
hand, there must be a reform'd discipline. Is that your new ruff,
sweet lady-bird? By my troth, 'tis most intricately rare.

MER. Good Jove, what reverend gentlewoman in years might this be?

CUP. 'Tis madam Moria, guardian of the nymphs; one that is not now
to be persuaded of her wit; she will think herself wise against all
the judgments that come. A lady made all of voice and air, talks

any thing of any thing. She is like one of your ignorant poetasters of the time, who, when they have got acquainted with a strange word, never rest till they have wrung it in, though it loosen the whole fabric of their sense.

MER. That was pretty and sharply noted, Cupid.

CUP. She will tell you, Philosophy was a fine reveller, when she was young, and a gallant, and that then, though she say it, she was thought to be the dame Dido and Helen of the court: as also, what a sweet dog she had this time four years, and how it was called Fortune; and that, if the Fates had not cut his thread, he had been a dog to have given entertainment to any gallant in this kingdom; and unless she had whelp'd it herself, she could not have loved a thing better in this world.

MER. O, I prithee no more; I am full of her.

CUP. Yes, I must needs tell you she composes a sack-posset well; and would court a young page sweetly, but that her breath is against it.

MER. Now, her breath or something more strong protect me from her! The other, the other, Cupid.

CUP. O, that's my lady and mistress, madam Philautia. She admires not herself for any one particularity, but for all: she is fair, and she knows it; she has a pretty light wit too, and she knows it; she can dance, and she knows that too; play at shuttle-cock, and that too: no quality she has, but she shall take a very particular knowledge of, and most lady-like commend it to you. You shall have her at any time read you the history of herself, and very subtilely run over another lady's sufficiencies to come to her own. She has a good superficial judgment in painting; and would seem to have so in poetry. A most complete lady in the opinion of some three beside herself.

PHI. Faith, how liked you my quip to Hedon, about the garter? Was't not witty?

MOR. Exceeding witty and integrate: you did so aggravate the jest withal.

PHI. And did I not dance movingly the last night?

MOR. Movingly! out of measure, in troth, sweet charge.

MER. A happy commendation, to dance out of measure!

MOR. Save only you wanted the swim in the turn: O! when I was at fourteen --

PHI. Nay, that's mine own from any nymph in the court, I'm sure on't; therefore you mistake me in that, guardian: both the swim and the trip are properly mine; every body will affirm it that has any judgment in dancing, I assure you.

PHA. Come now, Philautia, I am for you; shall we go?

PHI. Ay, good Phantaste: What! have you changed your head-tire?

PHA. Yes, faith; the other was so near the common, it had no extraordinary grace; besides, I had worn it almost a day, in good troth.

PHI. I'll be sworn, this is most excellent for the device, and rare; 'tis after the Italian print we look'd on t'other night.

PHA. 'Tis so: by this fan, I cannot abide any thing that savours the poor over-worn cut, that has any kindred with it; I must have variety, I: this mixing in fashion, I hate it worse than to burn juniper in my chamber, I protest.

PHI. And yet we cannot have a new peculiar court-tire, but these retainers will have it; these suburb Sunday-waiters; these courtiers for high days; I know not what I should call 'em --

PHA. O, ay, they do most pitifully imitate; but I have a tire a coming, i'faith, shall --

MOR. In good certain, madam, it makes you look most heavenly; but, lay your hand on your heart, you never skinn'd a new beauty more prosperously in your life, nor more metaphysically: look good lady, sweet lady, look.

PHI. 'Tis very clear and well, believe me. But if you had seen mine yesterday, when 'twas young, you would have -- Who's your doctor, Phantaste?

PHA. Nay, that's counsel, Philautia; you shall pardon me: yet I'll assure you he's the most dainty, sweet, absolute, rare man of the whole college. O! his very looks, his discourse, his behaviour, all he does is physic, I protest.

PHI. For heaven's sake, his name, good dear Phantaste?

PHA. No, no, no, no, no, no, believe me, not for a million of heavens: I will not make him cheap. Fie --

[EXEUNT PHANTASTE, MORIA, AND PHILAUTIA.]

CUP. There is a nymph too of a most curious and elaborate strain, light, all motion, an ubiquitary, she is every where, Phantaste --

MER. Her very name speaks her, let her pass. But are these, Cupid, the stars of Cynthia's court? Do these nymphs attend upon Diana?

CUP. They are in her court, Mercury, but not as stars; these never come in the presence of Cynthia. The nymphs that make her train are the divine Arete, Time, Phronesis, Thauma, and others of that high sort. These are privately brought in by Moria in this licentious time, against her knowledge; and, like so many meteors, will vanish when she appears.

ENTER PROSAITES SINGING, FOLLOWED BY GELAIA AND COS, WITH BOTTLES.

Come follow me, my wags, and say, as I say,
There's no riches but in rags, hey day, hey day:
You that profess this art, come away, come away,
And help to bear a part. Hey day, hey day, etc.

[MERCURY AND CUPID COME FORWARD.]

MER. What, those that were our fellow pages but now, so soon preferr'd to be yeomen of the bottles! The mystery, the mystery, good wags?

CUP. Some diet-drink they have the guard of.

PRO. No, sir, we are going in quest of a strange fountain, lately found out.

CUP. By whom?

COS. My master or the great discoverer, Amorphus.

MER. Thou hast well entitled him, Cos, for he will discover all he knows.

GEL. Ay, and a little more too, when the spirit is upon him.

PRO. O, the good travelling gentleman yonder has caused such a drought in the presence, with reporting the wonders of this new water, that all the ladies and gallants lie languishing upon the rushes, like so many pounded cattle in the midst of harvest, sighing one to another, and gasping, as if each of them expected a cock from the fountain to be brought into his mouth; and without we return quickly, they are all, as a youth would say, no better then a few trouts cast ashore, or a dish of eels in a sand-bag.

MER. Well then, you were best dispatch, and have a care of them. Come, Cupid, thou and I'll go peruse this dry wonder. [EXEUNT.]

ACT III

SCENE I. -- AN APARTMENT AT THE COURT.

ENTER AMORPHUS AND ASOTUS.

AMO. Sir, let not this discountenance or disgallant you a whit; you must not sink under the first disaster. It is with your young grammatical courtier, as with your neophyte player, a thing usual to be daunted at the first presence or interview: you saw, there was Hedon, and Anaides, far more practised gallants than yourself, who were both out, to comfort you. It is no disgrace, no more than for your adventurous reveller to fall by some inauspicious chance in his galliard, or for some subtle politic to undertake the bastinado, that the state might think worthily of him, and respect him as a man well beaten to the world. What? hath your tailor provided the property we spake of at your chamber, or no?

ASO. I think he has.

AMO. Nay, I entreat you, be not so flat and melancholic. Erect your mind: you shall redeem this with the courtship I will teach you against the afternoon. Where eat you to-day?

ASO. Where you please, sir; any where, I.

AMO. Come, let us go and taste some light dinner, a dish of sliced caviare, or so; and after, you shall practise an hour at your lodging some few forms that I have recall'd. If you had but so far gathered your spirits to you, as to have taken up a rush when you were out, and wagg'd it thus, or cleansed your teeth with it; or but turn'd aside, and feign'd some business to whisper with your page, till you had recovered yourself, or but found some slight stain in your stocking, or any other pretty invention, so it had been sudden, you might have come off with a most clear and courtly grace.

ASO. A poison of all! I think I was forespoke, I.

AMO. No, I must tell you, you are not audacious enough; you must frequent ordinaries a month more, to initiate yourself: in which time, it will not be amiss, if, in private, you keep good your acquaintance with Crites, or some other of his poor coat; visit his lodging secretly and often; become an earnest suitor to hear some of his labours.

ASO. O Jove! sir, I could never get him to read a line to me.

AMO. You must then wisely mix yourself in rank with such as you know can; and, as your ears do meet with a new phrase, or an acute jest, take it in: a quick nimble memory will lift it away, and, at your next public meal, it is your own.

ASO. But I shall never utter it perfectly, sir.

AMO. No matter, let it come lame. In ordinary talk you shall play it away, as you do your light crowns at primero: it will pass.

ASO. I shall attempt, sir.

AMO. Do. It is your shifting age for wit, and, I assure you, men must be prudent. After this you may to court, and there fall in, first with the waiting-woman, then with the lady. Put case they do retain you there, as a fit property, to hire coaches some pair of months, or so; or to read them asleep in afternoons upon some pretty pamphlet, to breathe you; why, it shall in time embolden you to some farther achievement: in the interim, you may fashion yourself to be careless and impudent.

ASO. How if they would have me to make verses? I heard Hedon spoke to for some.

AMO. Why, you must prove the aptitude of your genius; if you find none, you must hearken out a vein, and buy; provided you pay for the silence as for the work, then you may securely call it your own.

ASO. Yes, and I'll give out my acquaintance with all the best writers, to countenance me the more.

AMO. Rather seem not to know them, it is your best. Ay, be wise, that you never so much as mention the name of one, nor remember it mentioned; but if they be offer'd to you in discourse, shake your light head, make between a sad and a smiling face, pity some, rail at all, and commend yourself: 'tis your only safe and unsuspected course. Come, you shall look back upon the court again to-day, and be restored to your colours: I do now partly aim at the cause of your repulse -- which was ominous indeed -- for as you enter at the door, there is opposed to you the frame of a wolf in the hangings, which, surprising your eye suddenly, gave a false alarm to the heart; and that was it called your blood out of your face, and so routed the whole rank of your spirits: I beseech you labour to forget it. And remember, as I inculcated to you before, for your comfort, Hedon and Anaides. [EXEUNT.]

SCENE II. -- ANOTHER APARTMENT IN THE SAME.

ENTER HEDON AND ANAIDES.

HEDON. Heart, was there ever so prosperous an invention thus unluckily perverted and spoiled, by a whoreson book-worm, a candle-waster?

ANA. Nay, be not impatient, Hedon.

HED. 'Slight, I would fain know his name.

ANA. Hang him, poor grogan rascal! prithee think not of him: I'll send for him to my lodging, and have him blanketed when thou wilt, man.

HED. Ods so, I would thou couldst. Look, here he comes.

ENTER CRITES, AND WALKS IN A MUSING POSTURE AT THE BACK OF THE
STAGE.

Laugh at him, laugh at him; ha, ha, ha.

ANA. Fough! he smells all lamp-oil with studying by candle-light.

HED. How confidently he went by us, and carelessly! Never moved, nor stirred at any thing! Did you observe him?

ANA. Ay, a pox on him, let him go, dormouse: he is in a dream now. He has no other time to sleep, but thus when he walks abroad to take the air.

HED. 'Sprecious, this afflicts me more than all the rest, that we should so particularly direct our hate and contempt against him, and he to carry it thus without wound or passion! 'tis insufferable.

ANA. 'Slid, my dear Envy, if thou but say'st the word now, I'll undo him eternally for thee.

HED. How, sweet Anaides?

ANA. Marry, half a score of us get him in, one night, and make him pawn his wit for a supper.

HED. Away, thou hast such unseasonable jests! By this heaven, I wonder at nothing more than our gentlemen ushers, that will suffer a piece of serge or perpetuana to come into the presence: methinks they should, out of their experience, better distinguish the silken disposition of courtiers, than to let such terrible coarse rags mix with us, able to fret any smooth or gentle society to the threads with their rubbing devices.

ANA. Unless 'twere Lent, Ember-weeks, or fasting days, when the place is most penuriously empty of all other good outsides. D--n me, if I should adventure on his company once more, without a suit of buff to defend my wit! he does nothing but stab, the slave! How mischievously he cross'd thy device of the prophecy, there? and Moria, she comes without her muff too, and there my invention was lost.

HED. Well, I am resolved what I'll do.

ANA. What, my good spiritous spark?

HED. Marry, speak all the venom I can of him; and poison his reputation in every place where I come.

ANA. 'Fore God, most courtly.

HED. And if I chance to be present where any question is made of his sufficiencies, or of any thing he hath done private or public, I'll censure it slightly, and ridiculously.

ANA. At any hand beware of that; so thou may'st draw thine own judgment in suspect. No, I'll instruct thee what thou shalt do, and by a safer means: approve any thing thou hearest of his, to the

received opinion of it; but if it be extraordinary, give it from
him to some other whom thou more particularly affect'st; that's the
way to plague him, and he shall never come to defend himself.
'Slud, I'll give out all he does is dictated from other men, and
swear it too, if thou'lt have me, and that I know the time and
place where he stole it, though my soul be guilty of no such thing;
and that I think, out of my heart, he hates such barren shifts: yet
to do thee a pleasure and him a disgrace, I'll damn myself, or do
any thing.

HED. Gramercy, my dear devil; we'll put it seriously in practice,
i'faith. [EXEUNT HEDON AND ANAIDES.]

CRI. [COMING FORWARD.]
Do, good Detraction, do, and I the while
Shall shake thy spight off with a careless smile.
Poor piteous gallants! what lean idle slights
Their thoughts suggest to flatter their starv'd hopes!
As if I knew not how to entertain
These straw-devices; but, of force must yield
To the weak stroke of their calumnious tongues.
What should I care what every dor doth buz
In credulous ears? It is a crown to me
That the best judgments can report me wrong'd;
Them liars; and their slanders impudent.
Perhaps, upon the rumour of their speeches,
Some grieved friend will whisper to me; Crites,
Men speak ill of thee. So they be ill men,
If they spake worse, 'twere better: for of such
To be dispraised, is the most perfect praise.
What can his censure hurt me, whom the world
Hath censured vile before me! If good Chrestus,
Euthus, or Phronimus, had spoke the words,

They would have moved me, and I should have call'd
My thoughts and actions to a strict account
Upon the hearing: but when I remember,
'Tis Hedon and Anaides, alas, then
I think but what they are, and am not stirr'd.
The one a light voluptuous reveller,
The other, a strange arrogating puff,
Both impudent, and ignorant enough;
That talk as they are wont, not as I merit;
Traduce by custom, as most dogs do bark,
Do nothing out of judgment, but disease,
Speak ill, because they never could speak well.
And who'd be angry with this race of creatures?
What wise physician have we ever seen
Moved with a frantic man? the same affects
That he doth bear to his sick patient,
Should a right mind carry to such as these;
And I do count it a most rare revenge,
That I can thus, with such a sweet neglect,
Pluck from them all the pleasure of their malice;
For that's the mark of all their enginous drifts,
To wound my patience, howso'er they seem
To aim at other objects; which if miss'd,
Their envy's like an arrow shot upright,
That, in the fall, endangers their own heads.

ENTER ARETE.

ARE. What, Crites! where have you drawn forth the day,
You have not visited your jealous friends?

CRI. Where I have seen, most honour'd Arete,
The strangest pageant, fashion'd like a court,

(At least I dreamt I saw it) so diffused,
So painted, pied, and full of rainbow strains;
As never yet, either by time, or place,
Was made the food to my distasted sense;
Nor can my weak imperfect memory
Now render half the forms unto my tongue,
That were convolved within this thrifty room.
Here stalks me by a proud and spangled sir,
That looks three handfuls higher then his foretop;
Savours himself alone, is only kind
And loving to himself; one that will speak
More dark and doubtful than six oracles!
Salutes a friend, as if he had a stitch;
Is his own chronicle, and scarce can eat
For regist'ring himself; is waited on
By mimics, jesters, panders, parasites,
And other such like prodigies of men.
He past, appears some mincing marmoset
Made all of clothes and face; his limbs so set
As if they had some voluntary act
Without man's motion, and must move just so
In spight of their creation: one that weighs
His breath between his teeth, and dares not smile
Beyond a point, for fear t'unstarch his look;
Hath travell'd to make legs, and seen the cringe
Of several courts, and courtiers; knows the time
Of giving titles, and of taking walls;
Hath read court common-places; made them his:
Studied the grammar of state, and all the rules
Each formal usher in that politic school
Can teach a man. A third comes, giving nods
To his repenting creditors, protests
To weeping suitors, takes the coming gold

Of insolent and base ambition,
That hourly rubs his dry and itchy palms;
Which griped, like burning coals, he hurls away
Into the laps of bawds, and buffoons' mouths.
With him there meets some subtle Proteus, one
Can change, and vary with all forms he sees;
Be any thing but honest; serves the time;
Hovers betwixt two factions, and explores
The drifts of both; which, with cross face, he bears
To the divided heads, and is received
With mutual grace of either: one that dares
Do deeds worthy the hurdle or the wheel,
To be thought somebody; and is in sooth
Such as the satirist points truly forth,
That only to his crimes owes all his worth.

ARE. You tell us wonders, Crites.

CRI. This is nothing.
There stands a neophite glazing of his face,
Pruning his clothes, perfuming of his hair,
Against his idol enters; and repeats,
Like an unperfect prologue, at third music,
His part of speeches, and confederate jests,
In passion to himself. Another swears
His scene of courtship over; bids, believe him,
Twenty times ere they will; anon, doth seem
As he would kiss away his hand in kindness;
Then walks off melancholic, and stands wreath'd,
As he were pinn'd up to the arras, thus.
A third is most in action, swims, and frisks,
Plays with his mistress's paps, salutes her pumps;
Adores her hems, her skirts, her knots, her curls,

Will spend his patrimony for a garter,
Or the least feather in her bounteous fan.
A fourth, he only comes in for a mute;
Divides the act with a dumb show, and exit.
Then must the ladies laugh, straight comes their scene,
A sixth times worse confusion then the rest.
Where you shall hear one talk of this man's eye,
Another of his lip, a third, his nose,
A fourth commend his leg, a fifth, his foot,
A sixth, his hand, and every one a limb;
That you would think the poor distorted gallant
Must there expire. Then fall they in discourse
Of tires, and fashions, how they must take place,
Where they may kiss, and whom, when to sit down,
And with what grace to rise; if they salute,
What court'sy they must use; such cobweb stuff
As would enforce the common'st sense abhor
Th' Arachnean workers.

ARE. Patience, gentle Crites.
This knot of spiders will be soon dissolved,
And all their webs swept out of Cynthia's court,
When once her glorious deity appears,
And but presents itself in her full light:
'Till when, go in, and spend your hours with us,
Your honour'd friends. Time and Phronesis,
In contemplation of our goddess' name.
Think on some sweet and choice invention now,
Worthy her serious and illustrious eyes,
That from the merit of it we may take
Desired occasion to prefer your worth,
And make your service known to Cynthia.
It is the pride of Arete to grace

Her studious lovers; and, in scorn of time,
Envy, and ignorance, to lift their state
Above a vulgar height. True happiness
Consists not in the multitude of friends,
But in their worth, and choice. Nor would I have
Virtue a popular regard pursue:
Let them be good that love me, though but few.

CRI. I kiss thy hands, divinest Arete,
And vow myself to thee, and Cynthia. [EXEUNT.]

SCENE III. -- ANOTHER APARTMENT IN THE SAME.

ENTER AMORPHUS, FOLLOWED BY ASOTUS AND HIS TAILOR.

AMO. A little more forward: so, sir. Now go in, discloak yourself, and come forth. [EXIT ASOTUS.] Tailor; bestow thy absence upon us; and be not prodigal of this secret, but to a dear customer.

[EXIT TAILOR.]

RE-ENTER ASOTUS.

'Tis well enter'd sir. Stay, you come on too fast; your pace is too impetuous. Imagine this to be the palace of your pleasure, or place where your lady is pleased to be seen. First you present yourself, thus: and spying her, you fall off, and walk some two turns; in which time, it is to be supposed, your passion hath sufficiently whited your face, then, stifling a sigh or two, and closing your lips, with a trembling boldness, and bold terror, you advance yourself forward. Prove thus much, I pray you.

ASO. Yes, sir; -- pray Jove I can light on it! Here I come in, you say, and present myself?

AMO. Good.

ASO. And then I spy her, and walk off?

AMO. Very good.

ASO. Now, sir, I stifle, and advance forward?

AMO. Trembling.

ASO. Yes, sir, trembling; I shall do it better when I come to it. And what must I speak now?

AMO. Marry, you shall say; "Dear Beauty", or "sweet Honour" (or by what other title you please to remember her), "methinks you are melancholy". This is, if she be alone now, and discompanied.

ASO. Well, sir, I'll enter again; her title shall be, "My dear Lindabrides".

AMO. Lindabrides!

ASO. Ay, sir, the emperor Alicandroe's daughter, and the prince Meridian's sister, in "the Knight of the Sun"; she should have been married to him, but that the princess Claridiana --

AMO. O, you betray your reading.

ASO. Nay, sir, I have read history, I am a little humanitian.

Interrupt me not, good sir. "My dear Lindabrides, -- my dear Lindabrides, -- my dear Lindabrides, methinks you are melancholy".

AMO. Ay, and take her by the rosy finger'd hand.

ASO. Must I so: O! -- "My dear Lindabrides, methinks you are melancholy".

AMO. Or thus sir. "All variety of divine pleasures, choice sports, sweet music, rich fare, brave attire, soft beds, and silken thoughts, attend this dear beauty."

ASO. Believe me, that's pretty. "All variety of divine pleasures, choice sports, sweet music, rich fare, brave attire, soft beds, and silken thoughts, attend this dear beauty."

AMO. And then, offering to kiss her hand, if she shall coily recoil, and signify your repulse, you are to re-enforce yourself with,
"More than most fair lady,
Let not the rigour of your just disdain
Thus coarsely censure of your servant's zeal."
And withal, protest her to be the only and absolute unparallel'd creature you do adore, and admire, and respect, and reverence, in this court, corner of the world, or kingdom.

ASO. This is hard, by my faith. I'll begin it all again.

AMO. Do so, and I will act it for your lady.

ASO. Will you vouchsafe, sir? "All variety of divine pleasures, choice sports, sweet music, rich fare, brave attire, soft beds, and silken thoughts, attend this dear beauty."

AMO. So sir, pray you, away.

ASO. "More than most fair lady,
Let not the rigour of your just disdain
Thus coarsely censure of your servant's zeal;
I protest you are the only and absolute unapparell'd --

AMO. Unparallel'd.

ASO. Unparallel'd creature, I do adore, and admire, and respect, and reverence, in this corner of the world, or kingdom."

AMO. This is, if she abide you. But now, put the case she should be passant when you enter, as thus: you are to frame your gait thereafter, and call upon her, "lady, nymph, sweet refuge, star of our court." Then, if she be guardant, here; you are to come on, and, laterally disposing yourself, swear by her blushing and well-coloured cheek, the bright dye of her hair, her ivory teeth, (though they be ebony,) or some such white and innocent oath, to induce you. If regardant, then maintain your station, brisk and irpe, show the supple motion of your pliant body, but in chief of your knee, and hand, which cannot but arride her proud humour exceedingly.

ASO. I conceive you sir. I shall perform all these things in good time, I doubt not, they do so hit me.

AMO. Well sir, I am your lady; make use of any of these beginnings, or some other out of your own invention; and prove how you can hold up, and follow it. Say, say.

ASO. Yes sir. "My dear Lindabrides."

AMO. No, you affect that Lindabrides too much; and let me tell you it is not so courtly. Your pedant should provide you some parcels of French, or some pretty commodity of Italian, to commence with, if you would be exotic and exquisite.

ASO. Yes, sir, he was at my lodging t'other morning, I gave him a doublet.

AMO. Double your benevolence, and give him the hose too; clothe you his body, he will help to apparel your mind. But now, see what your proper genius can perform alone, without adjection of any other Minerva.

ASO. I comprehend you sir.

AMO. I do stand you, sir; fall back to your first place. Good, passing well: very properly pursued.

ASO. "Beautiful, ambiguous, and sufficient lady, what! are you all alone?"

AMO. "We would be, sir, if you would leave us."

ASO. "I am at your beauty's appointment, bright angel; but --"

AMO "What but?"

ASO. "No harm, more than most fair feature."

AMO. That touch relish'd well.

ASO. "But I protest --"

AMO. "And why should you protest?"

ASO. "For good will, dear esteem'd madam, and I hope your ladyship will so conceive of it:
And will, in time, return from your disdain,
And rue the suff'rance of our friendly pain."

AMO. O, that piece was excellent! If you could pick out more of these play-particles, and, as occasion shall salute you, embroider or damask your discourse with them, persuade your soul, it would most judiciously commend you. Come, this was a well-discharged and auspicious bout. Prove the second.

ASO. "Lady, I cannot ruffle it in red and yellow."

AMO. "Why if you can revel it in white, sir, 'tis sufficient."

ASO. "Say you so, sweet lady! Lan, tede, de, de, de, dant, dant, dant, dante. [SINGS AND DANCES.] No, in good faith, madam, whosoever told your ladyship so, abused you; but I would be glad to meet your ladyship in a measure."

AMO. "Me sir! Belike you measure me by yourself, then?"

ASO. "Would I might, fair feature."

AMO. "And what were you the better, if you might?"

ASO. "The better it please you to ask, fair lady."

AMO. Why, this was ravishing, and most acutely continued. Well, spend not your humour too much, you have now competently exercised your conceit: this, once or twice a day, will render you an accomplish'd, elaborate, and well-levell'd gallant. Convey in your courting-stock, we will in the heat of this go visit the nymphs' chamber.

ACT IV

SCENE I. -- AN APARTMENT IN THE PALACE.

ENTER PHANTASTE, PHILAUTIA, ARGURION, MORIA, AND CUPID.

PHA. I would this water would arrive once, our travelling friend so commended to us.

ARG. So would I, for he has left all us in travail with expectation of it.

PHA. Pray Jove, I never rise from this couch, if ever I thirsted more for a thing in my whole time of being a courtier.

PHI Nor I, I'll be sworn: the very mention of it sets my lips in a worse heat, than if he had sprinkled them with mercury. Reach me the glass, sirrah.

CUP. Here, lady.

MOR. They do not peel, sweet charge, do they?

PHI. Yes, a little, guardian.

MOR. O, 'tis an eminent good sign. Ever when my lips do so, I am sure to have some delicious good drink or other approaching.

ARG. Marry, and this may be good for us ladies, for it seems 'tis far fet by their stay.

MOR. My palate for yours, dear Honour, it shall prove most elegant I warrant you. O, I do fancy this gear that's long a coming, with an unmeasurable strain.

PHA. Pray thee sit down, Philautia; that rebatu becomes thee singularly.

PHI. Is it not quaint?

PHA. Yes faith. Methinks, thy servant Hedon is nothing so obsequious to thee, as he was wont to be: I know not how, he is grown out of his garb a-late, he's warp'd.

MOR. In trueness, and so methinks too; he is much converted.

PHI. Tut; let him be what he will, 'tis an animal I dream not of. This tire, methinks, makes me look very ingeniously, quick, and spirited; I should be some Laura, or some Delia, methinks.

MOR. As I am wise, fair Honours, that title she gave him, to be her Ambition, spoil'd him: before, he was the most propitious and observant young novice --

PHA. No, no, you are the whole heaven awry, guardian; 'tis the swaggering coach-horse Anaides draws with him there, has been the diverter of him.

PHI. For Cupid's sake speak no more of him; would I might never dare to look in a mirror again, if I respect ever a marmoset of 'em all, otherwise than I would a feather, or my shuttle-cock, to make sport with now and then.

PHA. Come sit down: troth, and you be good beauties, let's run over them all now: Which is the properest man amongst them? I say, the traveller, Amorphus.

PHI. O, fie on him, he looks like a Venetian trumpeter in the battle of Lepanto, in the gallery yonder; and speaks to the tune of a country lady that comes ever in the rearward or train of a fashion.

MOR. I should have judgment in a feature, sweet beauties.

PHA. A body would think so, at these years.

MOR. And I prefer another now, far before him, a million at least.

PHA. Who might that be, guardian?

MOR. Marry, fair charge, Anaides.

PHA. Anaides! you talk'd of a tune, Philautia; there's one speaks in a key, like the opening of some justice's gate, or a postboy's horn, as if his voice feared an arrest for some ill words it should give, and were loth to come forth.

PHI. Ay, and he has a very imperfect face.

PHA. Like a sea-monster, that were to ravish Andromeda from the rock.

PHI. His hands too great too, by at least a straw's breadth.

PHA. Nay, he has a worse fault than that too.

PHI. A long heel?

PHA. That were a fault in a lady, rather than him: no, they say he puts off the calves of his legs, with his stockings, every night.

PHI. Out upon him! Turn to another of the pictures, for love's sake. What says Argurion? Whom does she commend afore the rest?

CUP. I hope I have instructed her sufficiently for an answer. [ASIDE.]

MOR. Troth, I made the motion to her ladyship for one to-day, i'the presence, but it appear'd she was otherways furnished before: she would none.

PHA. Who was that Argurion?

MOR. Marry, the poor plain gentleman in the black there.

PHA. Who, Crites?

ARG. Ay, ay, he: a fellow that nobody so much as look'd upon, or regarded; and she would have had me done him particular grace.

PHA. That was a true trick of yourself, Moria, to persuade Argurion to affect the scholar.

ARG. Tut, but she shall be no chooser for me. In good faith, I like the citizen's son there, Asotus; methinks none of them all come near him.

PHA. Not Hedon?

ARG. Hedon! In troth no. Hedon's a pretty slight courtier, and he wears his clothes well, and sometimes in fashion; marry, his face is but indifferent, and he has no such excellent body. No, the other is a most delicate youth; a sweet face, a straight body, a well-proportion'd leg and foot, a white hand, a tender voice.

PHI. How now, Argurion!

PHA. O, you should have let her alone, she was bestowing a copy of him upon us. Such a nose were enough to make me love a man, now.

PHI. And then his several colours he wears; wherein he flourisheth changeably, every day.

PHA. O, but his short hair, and his narrow eyes!

PHI. Why she doats more palpably upon him than ever his father did upon her.

PHA. Believe me, the young gentleman deserves it. If she could doat more, 'twere not amiss. He is an exceeding proper youth, and would have made a most neat barber surgeon, if he had been put to it in time.

PHI. Say you so? Methinks he looks like a tailor already.

PHA. Ay, that had sayed on one of his customer's suits. His face is like a squeezed orange, or --

ARG. Well ladies, jest on: the best of you both would be glad of such a servant.

MOR. Ay, I'll be sworn would they, though he be a little shame-faced.

PHA. Shame-faced, Moria! out upon him. Your shame-faced servant is your only gull.

MOR. Go to, beauties, make much of time, and place, and occasion, and opportunity, and favourites, and things that belong to them, for I'll ensure you they will all relinquish; they cannot endure above another year; I know it out of future experience; and therefore take exhibition, and warning: I was once a reveller myself, and though I speak it, as mine own trumpet, I was then esteem'd --

PHI. The very march-pane of the court, I warrant you.

PHA. And all the gallants came about you like flies, did they not?

MOR. Go to, they did somewhat; that's no matter now.

PHA. Nay, good Moria, be not angry. Put case, that we four now had the grant from Juno, to wish ourselves into what happy estate we could, what would you wish to be, Moria?

MOR. Who, I! let me see now. I would wish to be a wise woman, and know all the secrets of court, city, and country. I would know what were done behind the arras, what upon the stairs, what in the garden, what in the nymphs' chamber, what by barge, and what by coach. I would tell you which courtier were scabbed and which not; which lady had her own face to lie with her a-nights and which not;

who put off their teeth with their clothes in court, who their
hair, who their complexion; and in which box they put it. There
should not a nymph, or a widow, be got with child in the verge, but
I would guess, within one or two, who was the right father, and in
what month it was gotten; with what words, and which way. I would
tell you which madam loved a monsieur, which a player, which a
page; who slept with her husband, who with her friend, who with her
gentleman-usher, who with her horse-keeper, who with her monkey,
and who with all; yes, and who jigg'd the cock too.

PHA. Fie, you'd tell all, Moria! If I should wish now, it should
be to have your tongue out. But what says Philautia? Who should
she be?

PHI. Troth, the very same I am. Only I would wish myself a little
more command and sovereignty; that all the court were subject to my
absolute beck, and all things in it depending on my look; as if
there were no other heaven but in my smile, nor other hell but in
my frown; that I might send for any man I list, and have his head
cut off when I have done with him, or made an eunuch if he denied
me; and if I saw a better face than mine own, I might have my
doctor to poison it. What would you wish, Phantaste?

PHA. Faith, I cannot readily tell you what: but methinks I should
wish myself all manner of creatures. Now I would be an empress,
and by and by a duchess; then a great lady of state, then one of
your miscellany madams, then a waiting-woman, then your citizen's
wife, then a coarse country gentlewoman, then a dairy-maid, then a
shepherd's lass, then an empress again, or the queen of fairies:
and thus I would prove the vicissitudes and whirl of pleasures
about and again. As I were a shepherdess, I would be piped and
sung to; as a dairy-wench, I would dance at maypoles, and make
syllabubs; as a country gentlewoman, keep a good house, and come up

to term to see motions; as a citizen's wife, to be troubled with a jealous husband, and put to my shifts; others' miseries should be my pleasures. As a waiting-woman, I would taste my lady's delights to her; as a miscellany madam, invent new tires, and go visit courtiers; as a great lady, lie a-bed, and have courtiers visit me; as a duchess, I would keep my state; and as an empress, I would do any thing. And, in all these shapes, I would ever be follow'd with the affections of all that see me. Marry, I myself would affect none; or if I did, it should not be heartily, but so as I might save myself in them still, and take pride in tormenting the poor wretches. Or, now I think on't, I would, for one year, wish myself one woman; but the richest, fairest, and delicatest in a kingdom, the very centre of wealth and beauty, wherein all lines of love should meet; and in that person I would prove all manner of suitors, of all humours, and of all complexions, and never have any two of a sort. I would see how love, by the power of his object, could work inwardly alike, in a choleric man and a sanguine, in a melancholic and a phlegmatic, in a fool and a wise man, in a clown and a courtier, in a valiant man and a coward; and how he could vary outward, by letting this gallant express himself in dumb gaze; another with sighing and rubbing his fingers; a third with play-ends and pitiful verses; a fourth, with stabbing himself, and drinking healths, or writing languishing letters in his blood; a fifth, in colour'd ribands and good clothes; with this lord to smile, and that lord to court, and the t'other lord to dote, and one lord to hang himself. And, then, I to have a book made of all this, which I would call the "Book of Humours," and every night read a little piece ere I slept, and laugh at it. -- Here comes Hedon.

ENTER HEDON, ANAIDES, AND MERCURY, WHO RETIRES WITH CUPID TO THE
BACK OF THE STAGE, WHERE THEY CONVERSE TOGETHER.

HED. Save you sweet and clear beauties! By the spirit that moves in me, you are all most pleasingly bestow'd, ladies. Only I can take it for no good omen, to find mine Honour so dejected.

PHI. You need not fear, sir; I did of purpose humble myself against your coming, to decline the pride of my Ambition.

HED. Fair Honour, Ambition dares not stoop; but if it be your sweet pleasure, I shall lose that title, I will, as I am Hedon, apply myself to your bounties.

PHI. That were the next way to dis-title myself of honour. O, no, rather be still Ambitious, I pray you.

HED. I will be any thing that you please, whilst it pleaseth you to be yourself, lady. Sweet Phantaste, dear Moria, most beautiful Argurion --

ANA. Farewell, Hedon.

HED. Anaides, stay, whither go you?

ANA. 'Slight, what should I do here? an you engross them all for your own use, 'tis time for me to seek out.

HED. I engross them! Away, mischief; this is one of your extravagant jests now, because I began to salute them by their names.

ANA. Faith, you might have spared us madam Prudence, the guardian there, though you had more covetously aim'd at the rest.

HED. 'Sheart, take them all, man: what speak you to me of aiming or covetous?

ANA. Ay, say you so! nay, then, have at them: Ladies, here's one hath distinguish'd you by your names already: It shall only become me to ask how you do.

HED. Ods so, was this the design you travail'd with?

PHA. Who answers the brazen head? it spoke to somebody.

ANA. Lady Wisdom, do you interpret for these puppets?

MOR. In truth, and sadness, honours, you are in great offence for this. Go to; the gentleman (I'll undertake with him) is a man of fair living, and able to maintain a lady in her two coaches a day, besides pages, monkeys, and paraquettoes, with such attendants as she shall think meet for her turn; and therefore there is more respect requirable, howso'er you seem to connive. Hark you, sir, let me discourse a syllable with you. I am to say to you, these ladies are not of that close and open behaviour as haply you may suspend; their carriage is well known to be such as it should be, both gentle and extraordinary.

MER. O, here comes the other pair.

ENTER AMORPHUS AND ASOTUS.

AMO. That was your father's love, the nymph Argurion. I would have you direct all your courtship thither; if you could but endear yourself to her affection, you were eternally engallanted.

ASO. In truth, sir! pray Phoebus I prove favoursome in her fair eyes.

AMO. All divine mixture, and increase of beauty to this bright bevy of ladies; and to the male courtiers, compliment and courtesy.

HED. In the behalf of the males, I gratify you, Amorphus.

PHA. And I of the females.

AMO. Succinctly return'd. I do vail to both your thanks, and kiss them; but primarily to yours, most ingenious, acute, and polite lady.

PHI. Ods my life, how he does all-to-bequalify her! "ingenious, acute", and "polite!" as if there was not others in place as ingenious, acute, and polite as she.

HED Yes, but you must know, lady, he cannot speak out of a dictionary method.

PHA. Sit down, sweet Amorphus. When will this water come, think you?

AMO. It cannot now be long, fair lady.

CUP. Now observe, Mercury.

ASO. How, most ambiguous beauty! love you? that I will, by this handkerchief.

MER. 'Slid, he draws his oaths out of his pocket.

ARG. But will you be constant?

ASO. Constant, madam! I will not say for constantness; but by this purse, which I would be loth to swear by, unless it were embroidered, I protest, more than most fair lady, you are the only absolute, and unparallel'd creature, I do adore, and admire, and respect, and reverence in this court, corner of the world, or kingdom. Methinks you are melancholy.

ARG. Does your heart speak all this?

ASO. Say you?

MER. O, he is groping for another oath.

ASO. Now by this watch -- I marle how forward the day is -- I do unfeignedly avow myself -- 'slight, 'tis deeper than I took it, past five -- yours entirely addicted, madam.

ARG. I require no more, dearest Asotus; henceforth let me call you mine, and in remembrance of me, vouchsafe to wear this chain and this diamond.

ASO. O lord, sweet lady!

CUP. There are new oaths for him. What! doth Hermes taste no alteration in all this?

MER. Yes, thou hast strook Argurion enamour'd on Asotus, methinks.

CUP. Alas, no; I am nobody, I; I can do nothing in this disguise.

MER. But thou hast not wounded any of the rest, Cupid.

CUP. Not yet; it is enough that I have begun so prosperously.

ARG. Nay, these are nothing to the gems I will hourly bestow upon thee; be but faithful and kind to me, and I will lade thee with my richest bounties: behold, here my bracelets from mine arms.

ASO. Not so, good lady, by this diamond.

ARG. Take 'em, wear 'em; my jewels, chain of pearl pendants, all I have.

ASO. Nay then, by this pearl you make me a wanton.

CUP. Shall not she answer for this, to maintain him thus in swearing?

MER. O no, there is a way to wean him from this, the gentleman may be reclaim'd.

CUP. Ay, if you had the airing of his apparel, coz, I think.

ASO. Loving! 'twere pity an I should be living else, believe me. Save you, sir, save you, sweet lady, save you, monsieur Anaides, save you, dear madam.

ANA. Dost thou know him that saluted thee, Hedon?

HED. No, some idle Fungoso, that hath got above the cupboard since yesterday.

ANA. 'Slud, I never saw him till this morning, and he salutes me as familiarly as if we had known together since the deluge, or the first year of Troy action.

AMO. A most right-handed and auspicious encounter. Confine yourself to your fortunes.

PHI. For sport's sake let's have some Riddles or Purposes, ho!

PHA. No, faith, your Prophecies are best, the t'other are stale.

PHI. Prophecies! we cannot all sit in at them; we shall make a confusion. No; what call'd you that we had in the forenoon?

PHA. Substantives, and adjectives, is it not, Hedon?

PHI. Ay that. Who begins?

PHA. I have thought; speak your adjectives, sirs.

PHI. But do not you change then.

PHA. Not I. Who says?

MOR. Odoriferous.

PHI. Popular.

ARG. Humble.

ANA. White-liver'd.

HED. Barbarous.

AMO. Pythagorical.

HED. Yours, signior.

ASO. What must I do, sir?

AMO. Give forth your adjective with the rest; as prosperous, good, fair, sweet, well --

HED. Anything that hath not been spoken.

ASO. Yes, sir, well-spoken shall be mine.

PHA. What, have you all done?

ALL. Ay.

PHA. Then the substantive is Breeches. Why "odoriferous" breeches, guardian?

MOR. Odoriferous, -- because odoriferous: that which contains most variety of savour and smell we say is most odoriferous; now breeches, I presume, are incident to that variety, and therefore odoriferous breeches.

PHA. Well, we must take it howsoever. Who's next? Philautia?

PHI. Popular.

PHA. Why "popular" breeches?

PHA. Marry, that is, when they are not content to be generally noted in court, but will press forth on common stages and brokers' stalls, to the public view of the world.

PHA. Good. Why "humble" breeches, Argurion?

ARG. Humble! because they use to be sat upon; besides, if you tie them not up, their property is to fall down about your heels.

MER. She has worn the breeches, it seems, which have done so.

PHA. But why "white-liver'd?"

ANA. Why! are not their linings white? Besides, when they come in swaggering company, and will pocket up any thing, may they not properly be said to be white-liver'd?

PHA. O yes, we must not deny it. And why "barbarous," Hedon?

HED. Barbarous! because commonly, when you have worn your breeches sufficiently, you give them to your barber.

AMO. That's good; but how "Pythagorical?"

PHI. Ay, Amorphus, why Pythagorical breeches?

AMO. O most kindly of all; 'tis a conceit of that fortune, I am bold to hug my brain for.

PHA. How is it, exquisite Amorphus?

AMO. O, I am rapt with it, 'tis so fit, so proper, so happy --

PHI. Nay, do not rack us thus.

AMO. I never truly relish'd myself before. Give me your ears. Breeches Pythagorical, by reason of their transmigration into several shapes.

MOR. Most rare, in sweet troth. Marry this young gentleman, for his well-spoken --

PHA. Ay, why "well-spoken" breeches?

ASO. Well-spoken! Marry, well-spoken, because -- whatsoever they speak is well-taken; and whatsoever is well-taken is well-spoken.

MOR. Excellent! believe me.

ASO. Not so, ladies, neither.

HED. But why breeches, now?

PHA. Breeches, "quasi" bear-riches; when a gallant bears all his riches in his breeches.

AMO. Most fortunately etymologised.

PHA. 'Nay, we have another sport afore this, of A thing done, and who did it, etc.

PHI. Ay, good Phantaste, let's have that: distribute the places.

PHA. Why, I imagine, A thing done; Hedon thinks, who did it; Moria, with what it was done; Anaides, where it was done; Argurion, when it was done; Amorphus, for what cause was it done; you, Philautia, what followed upon the doing of it; and this gentleman, who would have done it better. What? is it conceived about?

ALL. Yes, yes.

PHA. Then speak you, sir. "Who would have done it better?"

ASO. How! does it begin at me?

PHA. Yes, sir: this play is called the Crab, it goes backward.

ASO. May I not name myself?

PHI. If you please, sir, and dare abide the venture of it.

ASO. Then I would have done it better, whatever it is.

PHA. No doubt on't, sir: a good confidence. "What followed upon the act," Philautia?

PHI. A few heat drops, and a month's mirth.

PHA. "For what cause," Amorphus?

AMO. For the delight of ladies.

PHA. "When," Argurion?

ARG. Last progress.

PHA. "Where," Anaides?

ANA. Why, in a pair of pain'd slops.

PHA. "With what," Moria?

MOR. With a glyster.

PHA. "Who," Hedon?

HED. A traveller.

PHA. Then the thing done was, "An oration was made." Rehearse. An oration was made --

HED. By a traveller --

MOR. With a glyster --

ANA. In a pair of pain'd slops --

ARG. Last progress --

AMO. For the delight of ladies --

PHI. A few heat drops, and a month's mirth followed.

PHA. And, this silent gentleman would have done it better.

ASO. This was not so good, now.

PHI. In good faith, these unhappy pages would be whipp'd for staying thus.

MOR. Beshrew my hand and my heart else.

AMO. I do wonder at their protraction.

ANA. Pray Venus my whore have not discover'd herself to the rascally boys, and that be the cause of their stay.

ASO. I must suit myself with another page: this idle Prosaites will never be brought to wait well.

MOR. Sir, I have a kinsman I could willingly wish to your service, if you will deign to accept of him.

ASO. And I shall be glad, most sweet lady, to embrace him: Where is he?

MOR. I can fetch him, sir, but I would be loth to make you turn away your other page.

ASO. You shall not most sufficient lady; I will keep both: pray you let's go see him.

ARG. Whither goes my love?

ASO. I'll return presently, I go but to see a page with this lady.

[EXEUNT ASOTUS AND MORIA.]

ANA. As sure as fate, 'tis so: she has opened all: a pox of all cockatrices! D--n me, if she have play'd loose with me, I'll cut her throat within a hair's breadth, so it may be heal'd again.

MER. What, is he jealous of his hermaphrodite?

CUP. O, ay, this will be excellent sport.

PHI. Phantaste, Argurion! what, you are suddenly struck, methinks! For love's sake let's have some music till they come: Ambition, reach the lyra, I pray you.

HED. Anything to which my Honour shall direct me.

PHI. Come Amorphus, cheer up Phantaste.

AMO. It shall be my pride, fair lady, to attempt all that is in my power. But here is an instrument that alone is able to infuse soul into the most melancholic and dull-disposed creature upon earth. O, let me kiss thy fair knees. Beauteous ears attend it.

HED. Will you have "the Kiss" Honour?

PHI. Ay, good Ambition.

HEDON SINGS.

O, that joy so soon should waste!
Or so sweet a bliss
As a kiss
Might not for ever last!
So sugar'd, so melting, so soft, so delicious,
The dew that lies on roses,
When the morn herself discloses,
Is not so precious.
O rather than I would it smother,
Were I to taste such another;
It should be my wishing
That I might die with kissing.

HED. I made this ditty, and the note to it, upon a kiss that my Honour gave me; how like you it, sir?

AMO. A pretty air; in general, I like it well: but in particular, your long die-note did arride me most, but it was somewhat too long. I can show one almost of the same nature, but much before it, and not so long, in a composition of mine own. I think I have both the note and ditty about me.

HED. Pray you, sir, see.

AMO. Yes, there is the note; and all the parts, if I misthink not. I will read the ditty to your beauties here; but first I am to make you familiar with the occasion, which presents itself thus. Upon a time, going to take my leave of the emperor, and kiss his great hands, there being then present the kings of France and Arragon, the dukes of Savoy, Florence, Orleans, Bourbon, Brunswick, the Landgrave, Count Palatine; all which had severally feasted me; besides infinite more of inferior persons, as counts and others: it was my chance (the emperor detained by some exorbitant affair) to wait him the fifth part of an hour, or much near it. In which time, retiring myself into a bay-window, the beauteous lady Annabel, niece to the empress, and sister to the king of Arragon, who having never before eyed me, but only heard the common report of my virtue, learning, and travel, fell into that extremity of passion for my love, that she there immediately swooned: physicians were sent for, she had to her chamber, so to her bed; where, languishing some few days, after many times calling upon me, with my name in her lips, she expired. As that (I must mourningly say) is the only fault of my fortune, that, as it hath ever been my hap to be sued to, by all ladies and beauties, where I have come; so I never yet sojourn'd or rested in that place or part of the world, where some high-born, admirable, fair feature died not for my love.

MER. O, the sweet power of travel! -- Are you guilty of this, Cupid?

CUP. No, Mercury; and that his page Cos knows, if he were here present to be sworn.

PHI. But how doth this draw on the ditty, sir?

MER. O, she is too quick with him; he hath not devised that yet.

AMO. Marry, some hour before she departed, she bequeath'd to me this glove: which golden legacy, the emperor himself took care to send after me, in six coaches, cover'd all with black-velvet, attended by the state of his empire; all which he freely presented me with: and I reciprocally (out of the same bounty) gave to the lords that brought it: only reserving the gift of the deceased lady, upon which I composed this ode, and set it to my most affected instrument, the lyra.

Thou more then most sweet glove,
Unto my more sweet love,
Suffer me to store with kisses
This empty lodging, that now misses
The pure rosy hand, that wear thee,
Whiter than the kid that bare thee:
Thou art soft, but that was softer;
Cupid's self hath kiss'd it ofter
Than e'er he did his mother's doves.
Supposing her the queen of loves
That was thy mistress, BEST OF GLOVES.

MER. Blasphemy, blasphemy, Cupid!

CUP. I'll revenge it time enough, Hermes.

PHI. Good Amorphus, let's hear it sung.

AMO. I care not to admit that, since it pleaseth Philautia to request it.

HED. Here, sir.

AMO. Nay, play it, I pray you; you do well, you do well. [HE SINGS IT.] -- How like you it, sir?

HED. Very well, in troth.

AMO. But very well! O, you are a mere mammothrept in judgment, then. Why, do not observe how excellently the ditty is affected in every place? that I do not marry a word of short quantity to a long note? nor an ascending syllable to a descending tone? Besides, upon the word "best" there, you see how I do enter with an odd minum, and drive it through the brief; which no intelligent musician, I know, but will affirm to be very rare, extraordinary, and pleasing.

MER. And yet not fit to lament the death of a lady, for all this.

CUP. Tut, here be they will swallow anything.

PHA. Pray you, let me have a copy of it, Amorphus.

PHI. And me too; in troth I like it exceedingly.

AMO. I have denied it to princes; nevertheless to you, the true female twins of perfection, I am won to depart withal.

HED. I hope, I shall have my Honour's copy.

PHA. You are Ambitious in that, Hedon.

RE-ENTER ANAIDES.

AMO. How now, Anaides! what is it hath conjured up this distemperature in the circle of your face?

ANA. Why, what have you to do? A pox upon your filthy travelling face! hold your tongue.

HED. Nay, dost hear, Mischief?

ANA. Away, musk-cat!

AMO. I say to thee thou art rude, debauch'd, impudent, coarse, unpolish'd, a frapler, and base.

HED. Heart of my father, what a strange alteration has half a year's haunting of ordinaries wrought in this fellow! that came with a tufftaffata jerkin to town but the other day, and a pair of pennyless hose, and now he is turn'd Hercules, he wants but a club.

ANA. Sir, you with the pencil on your chin; I will garter my hose with your guts, and that shall be all. [EXIT.]

MER. 'Slid, what rare fireworks be here? flash, flash.

PHA. What is the matter Hedon? can you tell?

HED. Nothing, but that he lacks crowns, and thinks we'll lend him some to be friends.

RE-ENTER ASOTUS AND MORIA, WITH MORUS.

ASO. Come sweet lady, in good truth I'll have it, you shall not deny me. Morus, persuade your aunt I may have her picture, by any means.

MORUS. Yea, sir: good aunt now, let him have it; he will use me the better; if you love me do, good aunt.

MOR. Well, tell him he shall have it.

MORUS. Master, you shall have it, she says.

ASO. Shall I? thank her, good page.

CUP. What, has he entertained the fool?

MER. Ay, he'll wait close, you shall see, though the beggar hang off a while.

MORUS. Aunt, my master thanks you.

MOR. Call him hither.

MORUS. Yes; master.

MOR. Yes, in verity, and gave me this purse, and he has promised me a most fine dog; which he will have drawn with my picture, he says: and desires most vehemently to be known to your ladyships.

PHA. Call him hither, 'tis good groping such a gull.

MORUS. Master Asotus, master Asotus!

ASO. For love's sake, let me go: you see I am call'd to the ladies.

ARG. Wilt thou forsake me, then?

ASO. Od so! what would you have me do?

MOR. Come hither, master Asotus. -- I do ensure your ladyships, he is a gentleman of a very worthy desert: and of a most bountiful nature. -- You must shew and insinuate yourself responsible, and equivalent now to my commendment. -- Good honours grace him.

ASO. I protest, more then most fair ladies, "I do wish all variety of divine pleasures, choice sports, sweet music, rich fare, brave attire, soft beds, and silken thoughts, attend these fair beauties". Will it please your ladyship to wear this chain of pearl, and this diamond, for my sake?

ARG. O!

ASO. And you, madam, this jewel and pendants?

ARG. O!

PHA. We know not how to deserve these bounties, out of so slight merit, Asotus.

PHI. No, in faith, but there's my glove for a favour.

PHA. And soon after the revels, I will bestow a garter on you.

ASO. O lord, ladies! it is more grace than ever I could have hoped, but that it pleaseth your ladyships to extend. I protest it is enough, that you but take knowledge of my -- if your ladyships want embroidered gowns, tires of any fashion, rebatues, jewels, or carcanets, any thing whatsoever, if you vouchsafe to accept --

CUP. And for it they will help you to shoe-ties, and devices.

ASO. I cannot utter myself, dear beauties, but; you can conceive --

ARG. O!

PHA. Sir, we will acknowledge your service, doubt not -- henceforth, you shall be no more Asotus to us, but our goldfinch, and we your cages.

ASO. O Venus! madams! how shall I deserve this? if I were but made acquainted with Hedon, now, -- I'll try: pray you, away.

[TO ARGURION.]

MER. How he prays money to go away from him.

ASO. Amorphus, a word with you; here's a watch I would bestow upon you, pray you make me known to that gallant.

AMO. That I will, sir. -- Monsieur Hedon, I must entreat you to exchange knowledge with this gentleman.

HED. 'Tis a thing, next to the water, we expect, I thirst after, sir. Good monsieur Asotus.

ASO. Good monsieur Hedon, I would be glad to be loved of men of your rank and spirit, I protest. Please you to accept this pair of bracelets, sir; they are not worth the bestowing --

MER. O Hercules, how the gentleman purchases, this must needs bring Argurion to a consumption.

HED. Sir, I shall never stand in the merit of such bounty, I fear.

ASO. O Venus, sir; your acquaintance shall be sufficient. And if at any time you need my bill, or my bond --

ARG. O! O! [SWOONS.]

AMO. Help the lady there!

MOR. Gods-dear, Argurion! madam, how do you?

ARG. Sick.

PHA. Have her forth, and give her air.

ASO. I come again straight, ladies.

[EXEUNT ASOTUS, MORUS, AND ARGURION.]

MER. Well, I doubt all the physic he has will scarce recover her; she's too far spent.

RE-ENTER ANAIDES WITH GELAIA, PROSAITES, AND COS, WITH THE BOTTLES.

PHI. O here's the water come; fetch glasses, page.

GEL. Heart of my body, here's a coil, indeed, with your jealous humours! nothing but whore and bitch, and all the villainous swaggering names you can think on! 'Slid, take your bottle, and put it in your guts for me, I'll see you pox'd ere I follow you any longer.

ANA. Nay, good punk, sweet rascal; d--n me, if I am jealous now.

GEL. That's true, indeed, pray let's go.

MOR. What's the matter there?

GEL. 'Slight, he has me upon interrogatories, (nay, my mother shall know how you use me,) where I have been? and why I should stay so long? and how is't possible? and withal calls me at his pleasure I know not how many cockatrices, and things.

MOR. In truth and sadness, these are no good epitaphs Anaides, to bestow upon any gentlewoman; and I'll ensure you if I had known you would have dealt thus with my daughter, she should never have fancied you so deeply as she has done. Go to.

ANA. Why, do you hear, mother Moria? heart!

MOR. Nay, I pray you, sir, do not swear.

ANA. Swear! why? 'sblood, I have sworn afore now, I hope. Both you and your daughter mistake me. I have not honour'd Arete, that is held the worthiest lady in the court, next to Cynthia, with half that observance and respect, as I have done her in private, howsoever outwardly I have carried myself careless, and negligent. Come, you are a foolish punk, and know not when you are well employed. Kiss me, come on; do it, I say.

MOR. Nay, indeed, I must confess, she is apt to misprision. But I must have you leave it, minion.

RE-ENTER ASOTUS.

AMO. How now, Asotus! how does the lady?

ASO. Faith, ill. I have left my page with her, at her lodging.

HED. O, here's the rarest water that ever was tasted: fill him some.

PRO. What! has my master a new page?

MER. Yes, a kinsman of the lady Moria's: you must wait better now, or you are cashiered, Prosaites.

ANA. Come, gallants; you must pardon my foolish humour; when I am angry, that any thing crosses me, I grow impatient straight. Here, I drink to you.

PHI. O, that we had five or six bottles more of this liquor!

PHA. Now I commend your judgment, Amorphus: --
[KNOCKING WITHIN.]
Who's that knocks? look, page. [EXIT COS.]

MOR. O, most delicious; a little of this would make Argurion well.

PHA. O, no, give her no cold drink, by any means.

ANA. 'Sblood, this water is the spirit of wine, I'll be hang'd else.

RE-ENTER COS WITH ARETE.

COS. Here's the lady Arete, madam.

ARE. What, at your bever, gallants?

MOR. Will't please your ladyship to drink? 'tis of the New Fountain water.

ARE. Not I, Moria, I thank you. -- Gallants, you are for this night free to your peculiar delights; Cynthia will have no sports: when she is pleased to come forth, you shall have knowledge. In the mean time, I could wish you did provide for solemn revels, and some unlooked for device of wit, to entertain her, against she should vouchsafe to grace your pastimes with her presence.

AMO. What say you to a masque?

HED. Nothing better, if the project were new and rare.

ARE. Why, I'll send for Crites, and have his advice: be you ready in your endeavours: he shall discharge you of the inventive part.

PHA. But will not your ladyship stay?

ARE. Not now, Phantaste. [EXIT.]

PHI. Let her go, I pray you, good lady Sobriety, I am glad we are rid of her.

PHA. What a set face the gentlewoman has, as she were still going to a sacrifice!

PHI. O, she is the extraction of a dozen of Puritans, for a look.

MOR. Of all nymphs i' the court, I cannot away with her; 'tis the coarsest thing!

PHI. I wonder how Cynthia can affect her so above the rest. Here be they are every way as fair as she, and a thought, fairer, I trow.

PHA. Ay, and as ingenious and conceited as she.

MOR. Ay, and as politic as she, for all she sets such a forehead on't.

PHI. Would I were dead, if I would change to be Cynthia.

PHA. Or I.

MOR. Or I.

AMO. And there's her minion, Crites: why his advice more than Amorphus? Have I not invention afore him? Learning to better that invention above him? and infanted with pleasant travel --

ANA. Death, what talk you of his learning? he understands no more than a schoolboy; I have put him down myself a thousand times, by this air, and yet I never talk'd with him but twice in my life: you never saw his like. I could never get him to argue with me but once; and then because I could not construe an author I quoted at first sight, he went away, and laughed at me. By Hercules, I scorn him, as I do the sodden nymph that was here even now; his mistress,

Arete: and I love myself for nothing else.

HED. I wonder the fellow does not hang himself, being thus scorn'd and contemn'd of us that are held the most accomplish'd society of gallants.

MER. By yourselves, none else.

HED. I protest, if I had no music in me, no courtship; that I were not a reveller and could dance, or had not those excellent qualities that give a man life and perfection, but a mere poor scholar as he is, I think I should make some desperate way with myself; whereas now, -- would I might never breathe more, if I do know that creature in this kingdom with whom I would change.

CUP. This is excellent! Well, I must alter all this soon.

MER. Look you do, Cupid. The bottles have wrought, it seems.

ASO. O, I am sorry the revels are crost. I should have tickled it soon. I did never appear till then. 'Slid, I am the neatliest-made gallant i' the company, and have the best presence; and my dancing -- well, I know what our usher said to me last time I was at the school: Would I might have led Philautia in the measures, an it had been the gods' will! I am most worthy, I am sure.

RE-ENTER MORUS.

MORUS. Master, I can tell you news; the Lady kissed me yonder, and played with me, and says she loved you once as well as she does me, but that you cast her off.

ASO. Peace, my most esteemed page.

MORUS. Yes.

ASO. What luck is this, that our revels are dash'd, now was I beginning to glister in the very highway of preferment. An Cynthia had but seen me dance a strain, or do but one trick, I had been kept in court, I should never have needed to look towards my friends again.

AMO. Contain yourself, you were a fortunate young man, if you knew your own good; which I have now projected, and will presently multiply upon you. Beauties and valours, your vouchsafed applause to a motion. The humorous Cynthia hath, for this night, withdrawn the light of your delight.

PHA. 'Tis true, Amorphus: what may we do to redeem it?

AMO. Redeem that we cannot, but to create a new flame is in our power. Here is a gentleman, my scholar, whom, for some private reasons me specially moving, I am covetous to gratify with title of master in the noble and subtile science of courtship: for which grace, he shall this night, in court, and in the long gallery, hold his public act, by open challenge, to all masters of the mystery whatsoever, to play at the four choice and principal weapons thereof, viz., "the Bare Accost, the Better Regard, the Solemn Address," and "the Perfect Close." What say you?

ALL. Excellent, excellent, Amorphus.

AMO. Well, let us then take our time by the forehead: I will instantly have bills drawn, and advanced in every angle of the court. -- Sir, betray not your too much joy. -- Anaides, we must mix this gentleman with you in acquaintance, monsieur Asotus.

ANA. I am easily entreated to grace any of your friends, Amorphus.

ASO. Sir, and his friends shall likewise grace you, sir. Nay, I begin to know myself now.

AMO. O, you must continue your bounties.

ASO. Must I? Why, I'll give him this ruby on my finger. Do you hear sir? I do heartily wish your acquaintance, and I partly know myself worthy of it; please you, sir, to accept this poor ruby in a ring, sir. The poesy is of my own device, "Let this blush for me," sir.

ANA. So it must for me too, for I am not asham'd to take it.

MORUS. Sweet man! By my troth, master, I love you; will you love me too, for my aunt's sake? I'll wait well, you shall see. I'll still be here. Would I might never stir, but you are a fine man in these clothes; master, shall I have them when you have done with them?

ASO. As for that, Morus, thou shalt see more hereafter; in the mean time, by this air, or by this feather, I'll do as much for thee, as any gallant shall do for his page, whatsoever, in this court, corner of the world, or kingdom.

[EXEUNT ALL BUT THE PAGES.]

MER. I wonder this gentleman should affect to keep a fool: methinks he makes sport enough with himself.

CUP. Well, Prosaites, 'twere good you did wait closer.

PRO. Ay, I'll look to it; 'tis time.

COS. The revels would have been most sumptuous to-night, if they had gone forward. [EXIT.]

MER. They must needs, when all the choicest singularities of the court were up in pantofles; ne'er a one of them but was able to make a whole show of itself.

ASO. [WITHIN.] Sirrah, a torch, a torch!

PRO. O, what a call is there! I will have a canzonet made, with nothing in it but sirrah; and the burthen shall be, I come. [EXIT.]

MER. How now, Cupid, how do you like this change?

CUP. Faith, the thread of my device is crack'd, I may go sleep till the revelling music awake me.

MER. And then, too, Cupid, without you had prevented the fountain. Alas, poor god, that remembers not self-love to be proof against the violence of his quiver! Well, I have a plot against these prizers, for which I must presently find out Crites, and with his assistance pursue it to a high strain of laughter, or Mercury hath lost of his metal.

[EXEUNT.]

ACT V

SCENE I. -- THE SAME.

ENTER MERCURY AND CRITES.

MER. It is resolved on, Crites, you must do it.

CRI. The grace divinest Mercury hath done me,
In this vouchsafed discovery of himself,
Binds my observance in the utmost term
Of satisfaction to his godly will:
Though I profess, without the affectation
Of an enforced and form'd austerity,
I could be willing to enjoy no place
With so unequal natures.

MER. We believe it.
But for our sake, and to inflict just pains
On their prodigious follies, aid us now:
No man is presently made bad with ill.
And good men, like the sea, should still maintain
Their noble taste, in midst of all fresh humours
That flow about them, to corrupt their streams,
Bearing no season, much less salt of goodness.
It is our purpose, Crites, to correct,
And punish, with our laughter, this night's sport,
Which our court-dors so heartily intend:
And by that worthy scorn, to make them know
How far beneath the dignity of man
Their serious and most practised actions are.

CRI. Ay, but though Mercury can warrant out
His undertakings, and make all things good,
Out of the powers of his divinity,
Th' offence will be return'd with weight on me,
That am a creature so despised and poor;
When the whole court shall take itself abused
By our ironical confederacy.

MER. You are deceived. The better race in court,
That have the true nobility call'd virtue,
Will apprehend it, as a grateful right
Done to their separate merit; and approve
The fit rebuke of so ridiculous heads,
Who, with their apish customs and forced garbs,
Would bring the name of courtier in contempt,
Did it not live unblemish'd in some few,
Whom equal Jove hath loved, and Phoebus form'd
Of better metal, and in better mould.

CRI. Well, since my leader-on is Mercury,
I shall not fear to follow. If I fall,
My proper virtue shall be my relief,
That follow'd such a cause, and such a chief.

[EXEUNT.]

SCENE II. -- ANOTHER ROOM IN THE SAME.

ENTER ASOTUS AND AMORPHUS.

ASO. No more, if you love me, good master; you are incompatible to live withal: send me for the ladies!

AMO. Nay, but intend me.

ASO. Fear me not; I warrant you, sir.

AMO. Render not yourself a refractory on the sudden. I can allow, well, you should repute highly, heartily, and to the most, of your own endowments; it gives you forth to the world the more assured: but with reservation of an eye, to be always turn'd dutifully back upon your teacher.

ASO. Nay, good sir, leave it to me. Trust me with trussing all the points of this action, I pray. 'Slid, I hope we shall find wit to perform the science as well as another.

AMO. I confess you to be of an apted and docible humour. Yet there are certain punctilios, or (as I may more nakedly insinuate them) certain intrinsecate strokes and wards, to which your activity is not yet amounted, as your gentle dor in colours. For supposition, your mistress appears here in prize, ribanded with green and yellow; now, it is the part of every obsequious servant, to be sure to have daily about him copy and variety of colours, to be presently answerable to any hourly or half-hourly change in his mistress's revolution --

ASO. I know it, sir.

AMO. Give leave, I pray you -- which, if your antagonist, or player against you, shall ignorantly be without, and yourself can produce, you give him the dor.

ASO. Ay, ay, sir.

AMO. Or, if you can possess your opposite, that the green your mistress wears, is her rejoicing or exultation in his service; the yellow, suspicion of his truth, from her height of affection: and that he, greenly credulous, shall withdraw thus, in private, and from the abundance of his pocket (to displace her jealous conceit) steal into his hat the colour, whose blueness doth express trueness, she being not so, nor so affected; you give him the dor.

ASO. Do not I know it, sir?

AMO. Nay, good -- swell not above your understanding. There is yet a third dor in colours.

ASO. I know it too, I know it.

AMO. Do you know it too? what is it? make good your knowledge.

ASO. Why it is -- no matter for that.

AMO. Do it, on pain of the dor.

ASO. Why; what is't, say you?

AMO. Lo, you have given yourself the dor. But I will remonstrate to you the third dor, which is not, as the two former dors, indicative, but deliberative: as how? as thus. Your rival is, with a dutiful and serious care, lying in his bed, meditating how to observe his mistress, dispatcheth his lacquey to the chamber early, to know what her colours are for the day, with purpose to apply his wear that day accordingly: you lay wait before, preoccupy the chamber-maid, corrupt her to return false colours; he follows the fallacy, comes out accoutred to his believed instructions; your mistress smiles, and you give him the dor.

ASO. Why, so I told you, sir, I knew it.

AMO. Told me! It is a strange outrecuidance, your humour too much redoundeth.

ASO. Why, sir, what, do you think you know more?

AMO. I know that a cook may as soon and properly be said to smell well, as you to be wise. I know these are most clear and clean strokes. But then, you have your passages and imbrocatas in courtship; as the bitter bob in wit; the reverse in face or wry-mouth; and these more subtle and secure offenders. I will example unto you: Your opponent makes entry as you are engaged with your mistress. You seeing him, close in her ear with this whisper, "Here comes your baboon, disgrace him"; and withal stepping off, fall on his bosom, and turning to her, politely, aloud say, Lady, regard this noble gentleman, a man rarely parted, second to none in this court; and then, stooping over his shoulder, your hand on his breast, your mouth on his backside, you give him the reverse stroke, with this sanna, or stork's-bill, which makes up your wit's bob most bitter.

ASO. Nay, for heaven's sake, teach me no more. I know all as well -- 'Slid, if I did not, why was I nominated? why did you choose me? why did the ladies prick out me? I am sure there were other gallants. But me of all the rest! By that light, and, as I am a courtier, would I might never stir, but 'tis strange. Would to the lord the ladies would come once!

ENTER MORPHIDES.

MORP. Signior, the gallants and ladies are at hand. Are you ready, sir?

AMO. Instantly. Go, accomplish your attire: [EXIT ASOTUS.] Cousin Morphides, assist me to make good the door with your officious tyranny.

CITIZEN. [WITHIN.] By your leave, my masters there, pray you let's come by.

PAGES. [WITHIN.] You by! why should you come by more than we?

CITIZEN'S WIFE. [WITHIN.] Why, sir! because he is my brother that plays the prizes.

MORP. Your brother!

CITIZEN. [WITHIN.] Ay, her brother, sir, and we must come in.

TAILOR. [WITHIN.] Why, what are you?

CITIZEN. [WITHIN.] I am her husband, sir.

TAILOR. [WITHIN.] Then thrust forward your head.

AMO. What tumult is there?

MORP. Who's there? bear back there! Stand from the door!

AMO. Enter none but the ladies and their hang-byes. --

ENTER PHANTASTE, PHILAUTIA, ARGURION, MORIA, HEDON, AND ANAIDES,

INTRODUCING TWO LADIES.

Welcome beauties, and your kind shadows.

HED. This country lady, my friend, good signior Amorphus.

ANA. And my cockatrice here.

AMO. She is welcome.

THE CITIZEN, AND HIS WIFE, PAGES, ETC., APPEAR AT THE DOOR.

MORP. Knock those same pages there; and, goodman coxcomb the citizen, who would you speak withal?

WIFE. My brother.

AMO. With whom? your brother!

MORP. Who is your brother?

WIFE. Master Asotus.

AMO. Master Asotus! is he your brother? he is taken up with great persons; he is not to know you to-night.

RE-ENTER ASOTUS HASTILY.

ASO. O Jove, master! an there come e'er a citizen gentlewoman in my name, let her have entrance, I pray you: it is my sister.

WIFE. Brother!

CIT. [THRUSTING IN.] Brother, master Asotus!

ASO. Who's there?

WIFE. 'Tis I, brother.

ASO. Gods me, there she is! good master, intrude her.

MORP. Make place! bear back there!

ENTER CITIZEN'S WIFE.

AMO. Knock that simple fellow there.

WIFE. Nay, good sir, it is my husband.

MORP. The simpler fellow he. -- Away! back with your head, sir! [PUSHES THE CITIZEN BACK.]

ASO. Brother, you must pardon your non-entry: husbands are not allow'd here, in truth. I'll come home soon with my sister: pray you meet us with a lantern, brother. Be merry, sister: I shall make you laugh anon. [EXIT.]

PHA. Your prizer is not ready, Amorphus.

AMO. Apprehend your places; he shall be soon, and at all points.

ANA. Is there any body come to answer him? shall we have any sport?

AMO. Sport of importance; howsoever, give me the gloves.

HED. Gloves! why gloves, signior?

PHI. What's the ceremony?

AMO. [DISTRIBUTING GLOVES.] Beside their received fitness, at all prizes, they are here properly accommodate to the nuptials of my scholar's 'haviour to the lady Courtship. Please you apparel your hands. Madam Phantaste, madam Philautia, guardian, signior Hedon, signior Anaides, gentlemen all, ladies.

ALL. Thanks, good Amorphus.

AMO. I will now call forth my provost, and present him. [EXIT.]

ANA. Heart! why should not we be masters as well as he?

HED. That's true, and play our masters' prizes as well as the t'other?

MOR. In sadness, for using your court-weapons, methinks you may.

PHA. Nay, but why should not we ladies play our prizes, I pray? I see no reason but we should take them down at their own weapons.

PHI. Troth, and so we may, if we handle them well.

WIFE. Ay, indeed, forsooth, madam, if 'twere in the city, we would think foul scorn but we would, forsooth.

PHA. Pray you, what should we call your name?

WIFE. My name is Downfall.

HED. Good mistress Downfall! I am sorry your husband could not get in.

WIFE. 'Tis no matter for him, sir.

ANA. No, no, she has the more liberty for herself.

[A FLOURISH.]

PHA. Peace, peace! they come.

RE-ENTER AMORPHUS, INTRODUCING ASOTUS IN A FULL-DRESS SUIT.

AMO. So, keep up your ruff; the tincture of your neck is not all so pure, but it will ask it. Maintain your sprig upright; your cloke on your half-shoulder falling; so: I will read your bill, advance it, and present you. -- Silence!

"Be it known to all that profess courtship, by these presents (from the white satin reveller, to the cloth of tissue and bodkin) that we, Ulysses-Polytropus-Amorphus, master of the noble and subtile science of courtship, do give leave and licence to our provost, Acolastus-Polypragmon-Asotus, to play his master's prize, against all masters whatsoever, in this subtile mystery, at these four, the choice and most cunning weapons of court-compliment, viz. the BARE ACCOST; the BETTER REGARD; the SOLEMN ADDRESS; and the PERFECT CLOSE. These are therefore to give notice to all comers, that he, the said Acolastus-Polypragmon-Asotus, is here present (by the help of his mercer, tailor, milliner, sempster, and so forth) at his designed hour, in this fair gallery, the present day of this present month, to perform and do his uttermost for the achievement and bearing away of the prizes, which are these: viz. For the

Bare Accost, two wall-eyes in a face forced: for the Better Regard, a face favourably simpering, with a fan waving: for the Solemn Address, two lips wagging, and never a wise word: for the Perfect Close, a wring by the hand, with a banquet in a corner. And Phoebus save Cynthia!"

Appeareth no man yet, to answer the prizer? no voice? -- Music, give them their summons.

[MUSIC.]

PHA. The solemnity of this is excellent.

AMO. Silence! Well, I perceive your name is their terror, and keepeth them back.

ASO. I'faith, master, let's go; no body comes. 'Victus, victa, victum; victi, victae, victi -- let's be retrograde.

AMO. Stay. That were dispunct to the ladies. Rather ourself shall be your encounter. Take your state up to the wall; and, lady, [LEADING MORIA TO THE STATE.] may we implore you to stand forth, as first term or bound to our courtship.

HED. 'Fore heaven, 'twill shew rarely.

AMO. Sound a charge. [A CHARGE.]

ANA. A pox on't! Your vulgar will count this fabulous and impudent now: by that candle, they'll never conceit it.

[THEY ACT THEIR ACCOST SEVERALLY TO MORIA.]

PHA. Excellent well! admirable!

PHI. Peace!

HED. Most fashionably, believe it.

PHI. O, he is a well-spoken gentleman.

PHA. Now the other.

PHI. Very good.

HED. For a scholar, Honour.

ANA. O, 'tis too Dutch. He reels too much. [A FLOURISH.]

HED. This weapon is done.

AMO. No, we have our two bouts at every weapon; expect.

CRI. [WITHIN.] Where be these gallants, and their brave prizer here?

MORP. Who's there? bear back; keep the door.

ENTER CRITES, INTRODUCING MERCURY FANTASTICALLY DRESSED.

AMO. What are you, sir?

CRI. By your license, grand-master. -- Come forward, sir.
[TO MERCURY.]

ANA. Heart! who let in that rag there amongst us? Put him out, an impecunious creature.

HED. Out with him.

MORP. Come, sir.

AMO. You must be retrograde.

CRI. Soft, sir, I am truchman, and do flourish before this monsieur, or French-behaved gentleman, here; who is drawn hither by report of your chartels, advanced in court, to prove his fortune with your prizer, so he may have fair play shewn him, and the liberty to choose his stickler.

AMO. Is he a master?

CRI. That, sir, he has to shew here; and confirmed under the hands of the most skilful and cunning complimentaries alive: Please you read, sir. [GIVES HIM A CERTIFICATE.]

AMO. What shall we do?

ANA. Death! disgrace this fellow in the black stuff, whatever you do.

AMO. Why, but he comes with the stranger.

HED. That's no matter: he is our own countryman.

ANA. Ay, and he is a scholar besides. You may disgrace him here with authority.

AMO. Well, see these first.

ASO. Now shall I be observed by yon scholar, till I sweat again; I would to Jove it were over.

CRI. [TO MERCURY.] Sir, this is the wight of worth, that dares you to the encounter. A gentleman of so pleasing and ridiculous a carriage; as, even standing, carries meat in the mouth, you see; and, I assure you, although no bred courtling, yet a most particular man, of goodly havings, well-fashion'd 'haviour, and of as hardened and excellent a bark as the most naturally qualified amongst them, inform'd, reform'd, and transform'd, from his original citycism; by this elixir, or mere magazine of man. And, for your spectators, you behold them what they are: the most choice particulars in court: this tells tales well; this provides coaches; this repeats jests; this presents gifts; this holds up the arras; this takes down from horse; this protests by this light; this swears by that candle; this delighteth; this adoreth: yet all but three men. Then, for your ladies, the most proud, witty creatures, all things apprehending, nothing understanding, perpetually laughing, curious maintainers of fools, mercers, and minstrels, costly to be kept, miserably keeping, all disdaining but their painter and apothecary, 'twixt whom and them there is this reciprock commerce, their beauties maintain their painters, and their painters their beauties.

MER. Sir, you have plaid the painter yourself, and limn'd them to the life. I desire to deserve before them.

AMO. [RETURNING THE CERTIFICATE.] This is authentic. We must resolve to entertain the monsieur, howsoever we neglect him.

HED. Come, let's all go together, and salute him.

ANA. Content, and not look on the other.

AMO. Well devised; and a most punishing disgrace.

HED. On.

AMO. Monsieur, we must not so much betray ourselves to discourtship, as to suffer you to be longer unsaluted: please you to use the state ordain'd for the opponent; in which nature, without envy, we receive you.

HED. And embrace you.

ANA. And commend us to you, sir.

PHI. Believe it, he is a man of excellent silence.

PHA. He keeps all his wit for action.

ANA. This hath discountenanced our scholaris, most richly.

HED. Out of all emphasis. The monsieur sees we regard him not.

AMO. Hold on; make it known how bitter a thing it is not to be look'd on in court.

HED. 'Slud, will he call him to him yet! Does not monsieur perceive our disgrace?

ANA. Heart! he is a fool, I see. We have done ourselves wrong to grace him.

HED. 'Slight, what an ass was I to embrace him!

CRI. Illustrious and fearful judges --

HED. Turn away, turn away.

CRI. It is the suit of the strange opponent (to whom you ought not to turn your tails, and whose noses I must follow) that he may have the justice, before he encounter his respected adversary, to see some light stroke of his play, commenced with some other.

HED. Answer not him, but the stranger: we will not believe him.

AMO. I will demand him, myself.

CRI. O dreadful disgrace, if a man were so foolish to feel it.

AMO. Is it your suit, monsieur, to see some prelude of my scholar? Now, sure the monsieur wants language --

HED. And take upon him to be one of the accomplished! 'Slight, that's a good jest; would we could take him with that nullity. -- "Non sapete voi parlar' Italiano?"

ANA. 'Sfoot, the carp has no tongue.

CRI. Signior, in courtship, you are to bid your abettors forbear, and satisfy the monsieur's request.

AMO. Well, I will strike him more silent with admiration, and terrify his daring hither. He shall behold my own play with my scholar. Lady, with the touch of your white hand, let me reinstate you. [LEADS MORIA BACK TO THE STATE.] Provost, [TO ASOTUS.] begin to me at the "Bare Accost". [A CHARGE.] Now, for the honour of my discipline.

HED. Signior Amorphus, reflect, reflect; what means he by that mouthed wave?

CRI. He is in some distaste of your fellow disciple.

MER. Signior, your scholar might have played well still, if he could have kept his seat longer; I have enough of him, now. He is a mere piece of glass, I see through him by this time.

AMO. You come not to give us the scorn, monsieur?

MER. Nor to be frighted with a face, signior. I have seen the lions. You must pardon me. I shall be loth to hazard a reputation with one that has not a reputation to lose.

AMO. How!

CRI. Meaning your pupil, sir.

ANA. This is that black devil there.

AMO. You do offer a strange affront, monsieur.

CRI. Sir, he shall yield you all the honour of a competent adversary, if you please to undertake him.

MER. I am prest for the encounter.

AMO. Me! challenge me!

ASO. What, my master, sir! 'Slight, monsieur, meddle with me, do you hear: but do not meddle with my master.

MER. Peace, good squib, go out.

CRI. And stink, he bids you.

ASO. Master!

AMO. Silence! I do accept him. Sit you down and observe. Me! he never profest a thing at more charges. -- Prepare yourself sir. -- Challenge me! I will prosecute what disgrace my hatred can dictate to me.

CRI. How tender a traveller's spleen is! Comparison to men that deserve least, is ever most offensive.

AMO. You are instructed in our chartel, and know our weapons?

MER. I appear not without their notice, sir.

ASO. But must I lose the prizes, master?

AMO. I will win them for you; be patient. -- Lady, [TO MORIA.] vouchsafe the tenure of this ensign. -- Who shall be your stickler?

MER. Behold him. [POINTS TO CRITES.]

AMO. I would not wish you a weaker. -- Sound, musics. -- I provoke you at the Bare Accost. [A CHARGE.]

PHA. Excellent comely!

CRI. And worthily studied. This is the exalted foretop.

HED. O, his leg was too much produced.

ANA. And his hat was carried scurvily.

PHI. Peace; let's see the monsieur's Accost: Rare!

PHA. Sprightly and short.

ANA. True, it is the French courteau: he lacks but to have his nose slit.

HED. He does hop. He does bound too much. [A FLOURISH.]

AMO. The second bout, to conclude this weapon. [A CHARGE.]

PHA. Good, believe it!

PHI. An excellent offer!

CRI. This is called the solemn band-string.

HED. Foh, that cringe was not put home.

ANA. He makes a face like a stabb'd Lucrece.

ASO. Well, he would needs take it upon him, but would I had done it for all this. He makes me sit still here, like a baboon as I am.

CRI. Making villainous faces.

PHI. See, the French prepares it richly.

CRI. Ay, this is ycleped the Serious Trifle.

ANA. 'Slud, 'tis the horse-start out o' the brown study.

CRI. Rather the bird-eyed stroke, sir. Your observance is too blunt, sir. [A FLOURISH.]

AMO. Judges, award the prize. Take breath, sir. This bout hath been laborious.

ASO. And yet your critic, or your besongno, will think these things foppery, and easy, now!

CRI. Or rather mere lunacy. For would any reasonable creature make these his serious studies and perfections, much less, only live to these ends? to be the false pleasure of a few, the true love of none, and the just laughter of all?

HED. We must prefer the monsieur, we courtiers must be partial.

ANA. Speak, guardian. Name the prize, at the Bare Accost.

MOR. A pair of wall-eyes in a face forced.

ANA. Give the monsieur. Amorphus hath lost his eyes.

AMO. I! Is the palate of your judgment down? Gentles, I do appeal.

ASO. Yes, master, to me: the judges be fools.

ANA. How now, sir! tie up your tongue, mungrel. He cannot

appeal.

ASO. Say, you sir?

ANA. Sit you still, sir.

ASO. Why, so I do; do not I, I pray you?

MER. Remercie, madame, and these honourable censors.

AMO. Well, to the second weapon, the "Better Regard". I will encounter you better. Attempt.

HED. Sweet Honour.

PHI. What says my good Ambition?

HED. Which take you at this next weapon? I lay a Discretion with you on Amorphus's head.

PHI. Why, I take the French-behaved gentleman.

HED. 'Tis done, a Discretion.

CRI. A Discretion! A pretty court-wager! Would any discreet person hazard his wit so?

PHA. I'll lay a Discretion with you, Anaides.

ANA. Hang 'em, I'll not venture a doit of Discretion on either of their heads.

CRI. No, he should venture all then.

ANA. I like none of their plays. [A CHARGE.]

HED. See, see! this is strange play!

ANA. 'Tis too full of uncertain motion. He hobbles too much.

CRI. 'Tis call'd your court-staggers, sir.

HED. That same fellow talks so now he has a place!

ANA. Hang him! neglect him.

MER. "Your good ladyship's affectioned."

WIFE. Ods so! they speak at this weapon, brother.

ASO. They must do so, sister; how should it be the Better Regard, else?

PHA. Methinks he did not this respectively enough.

PHI. Why, the monsieur but dallies with him.

HED. Dallies! 'Slight, see! he'll put him to't in earnest. -- Well done, Amorphus!

ANA. That puff was good indeed.

CRI. Ods me! this is desperate play: he hits himself o' the shins.

HED. An he make this good through, he carries it, I warrant him.

CRI. Indeed he displays his feet rarely.

HED. See, see! he does the respective leer damnably well.

AMO. "The true idolater of your beauties shall never pass their deities unadored: I rest your poor knight."

HED. See, now the oblique leer, or the Janus: he satisfies all with that aspect most nobly. [A FLOURISH.]

Cri. And most terribly he comes off; like your rodomontado.

PHA. How like you this play, Anaides?

ANA. Good play; but 'tis too rough and boisterous.

AMO. I will second it with a stroke easier, wherein I will prove his language. [A CHARGE.]

ANA. This is filthy, and grave, now.

HED. O, 'tis cool and wary play. We must not disgrace our own camerade too much.

AMO. "Signora, ho tanto obligo per le favore resciuto da lei; che veramente desidero con tutto il core, a remunerarla in parte: e sicurative, signora mea cara, che io sera sempre pronto a servirla, e honorarla. Bascio le mane de vo' signoria."

CRI. The Venetian dop this.

PHA. Most unexpectedly excellent! The French goes down certain.

ASO. As buckets are put down into a well;
Or as a school-boy --

CRI. Truss up your simile, jack-daw, and observe.

HED. Now the monsieur is moved.

ANA. Bo-peep!

HED. O, most antick.

CRI. The French quirk, this sir.

ANA. Heart, he will over-run her.

MER. "Madamoyselle, Je voudroy que pouvoy monstrer mon affection, mais je suis tant malhereuse, ci froid, ci layd, ci -- Je ne scay qui de dire -- excuse moi, Je suis tout vostre." [A FLOURISH.]

PHI. O brave and spirited! he's a right Jovialist.

PHA. No, no: Amorphus's gravity outweighs it.

CRI. And yet your lady, or your feather, would outweigh both.

ANA. What's the prize, lady, at this Better Regard?

MOR. A face favourably simpering, and a fan waving.

ANA. They have done doubtfully. Divide. Give the favourable face to the signior, and the light wave to the monsieur.

AMO. You become the simper well, lady.

MER. And the wag better.

AMO. Now, to our "Solemn Address." Please the well-graced Philautia to relieve the lady sentinel; she hath stood long.

PHI. With all my heart; come, guardian, resign your place.

[MORIA COMES FROM THE STATE.]

AMO. Monsieur, furnish yourself with what solemnity of ornament you think fit for this third weapon; at which you are to shew all the cunning of stroke your devotion can possibly devise.

MER. Let me alone, sir. I'll sufficiently decipher your amorous solemnities. -- Crites, have patience. See, if I hit not all their practic observance, with which they lime twigs to catch their fantastic lady-birds.

CRI. Ay, but you should do more charitably to do it more openly, that they might discover themselves mock'd in these monstrous affections. [A CHARGE.]

MER. Lackey, where's the tailor?

ENTER TAILOR, BARBER, PERFUMER, MILLINER, JEWELLER, AND FEATHER-MAKER.

TAI. Here, sir.

HED. See, they have their tailor, barber, perfumer, milliner, jeweller, feather-maker, all in common!

[THEY MAKE THEMSELVES READY ON THE STAGE.]

ANA. Ay, this is pretty.

AMO. Here is a hair too much, take it off. Where are thy mullets?

MER. Is this pink of equal proportion to this cut, standing off this distance from it?

TAI. That it is, sir.

MER. Is it so, sir? You impudent poltroon, you slave, you list, you shreds, you -- BEATS THE TAILOR.]

HED. Excellent! This was the best yet.

ANA. Why, we must use our tailors thus: this is our true magnanimity.

MER. Come, go to, put on; we must bear with you for the times' sake.

AMO. Is the perfume rich in this jerkin?

PER. Taste, smell; I assure you, sir, pure benjamin, the only spirited scent that ever awaked a Neapolitan nostril. You would wish yourself all nose for the love on't. I frotted a jerkin for a new-revenued gentleman yielded me three-score crowns but this morning, and the same titillation.

AMO. I savour no sampsuchine in it.

PER. I am a Nulli-fidian, if there be not three-thirds of a scruple more of sampsuchinum in this confection, than ever I put in any. I'll tell you all the ingredients, sir.

AMO. You shall be simple to discover your simples.

PER. Simple! why, sir? What reck I to whom I discover? I have it in musk, civet, amber, Phoenicobalanus, the decoction of turmerick, sesana, nard, spikenard, calamus odoratus, stacte, opobalsamum, amomum, storax, ladanum, aspalathum, opoponax, oenanthe. And what of all these now? what are you the better? Tut, it is the sorting, and the dividing, and the mixing, and the tempering, and the searching, and the decocting, that makes the fumigation and the suffumigation.

AMO. Well, indue me with it.

PER. I will, sir.

HED. An excellent confection.

CRI. And most worthy a true voluptuary, Jove! what a coil these musk-worms take to purchase another's delight? for themselves, who bear the odours, have ever the least sense of them. Yet I do like better the prodigality of jewels and clothes, whereof one passeth to a man's heirs; the other at least wears out time. This presently expires, and, without continual riot in reparation, is lost: which whoso strives to keep, it is one special argument to me, that, affecting to smell better than other men, he doth indeed smell far worse.

MER. I know you will say, it sits well, sir.

TAI. Good faith, if it do not, sir, let your mistress be judge.

MER. By heaven, if my mistress do not like it, I'll make no more conscience to undo thee, than to undo an oyster.

TAI. Believe it, there's ne'er a mistress in the world can mislike it.

MER. No, not goodwife tailor, your mistress; that has only the judgment to heat your pressing-tool. But for a court-mistress that studies these decorums, and knows the proportion of every cut to a hair, knows why such a colour is cut upon such a colour, and when a satin is cut upon six taffataes, will look that we should dive into the depth of the cut -- Give me my scarf. Shew some ribands, sirrah. Have you the feather?

FEAT. Ay, sir.

MER. Have you the jewel?

JEW. Yes, sir.

MER. What must I give for the hire on't?

JEW. You shall give me six crowns, sir.

MER. Six crowns! By heaven, 'twere a good deed to borrow it of thee to shew, and never let thee have it again.

JEW. I hope your worship will not do so, sir.

MER. By Jove, sir, there be such tricks stirring, I can tell you, and worthily too. Extorting knaves, that live by these court-decorums, and yet -- What's your jewel worth, I pray?

JEW. A hundred crowns, sir.

MER. A hundred crowns, and six for the loan on't an hour! what's that in the hundred for the year? These impostors would not be hang'd! Your thief is not comparable to them, by Hercules. Well, put it in, and the feather; you will have it and you shall, and the pox give you good on't!

AMO. Give me my confects, my moscadini, and place those colours in my hat.

MER. These are Bolognian ribands, I warrant you.

MIL. In truth, sir, if they be not right Granado silk --

MER. A pox on you, you'll all say so.

MIL. You give me not a penny, sir.

MER. Come, sir, perfume my devant;
"May it ascend, like solemn sacrifice,
Into the nostrils of the Queen of Love!"

HED. Your French ceremonies are the best.

ANA. Monsieur, signior, your Solemn Address is too long; the ladies long to have you come on.

AMO. Soft, sir, our coming on is not so easily prepared. Signior Fig!

PER. Ay, sir.

AMO. Can you help my complexion, here?

PER. O yes, sir, I have an excellent mineral fucus for the purpose. The gloves are right, sir; you shall bury them in a muck-hill, a draught, seven years, and take them out and wash them, they shall still retain their first scent, true Spanish. There's ambre in the umbre.

MER. Your price, sweet Fig?

PER. Give me what you will, sir; the signior pays me two crowns a pair; you shall give me your love, sir.

MER. My love! with a pox to you, goodman Sassafras.

PER. I come, sir. There's an excellent diapasm in a chain, too, if you like it.

AMO. Stay, what are the ingredients to your fucus?

PER. Nought but sublimate and crude mercury, sir, well prepared and dulcified, with the jaw-bones of a sow, burnt, beaten, and searced.

AMO. I approve it. Lay it on.

MER. I'll have your chain of pomander, sirrah; what's your price?

PER. We'll agree, monsieur; I'll assure you it was both decocted and dried where no sun came, and kept in an onyx ever since it was balled.

MER. Come, invert my mustachio, and we have done.

AMO. 'Tis good.

BAR. Hold still, I pray you, sir.

PER. Nay, the fucus is exorbitant, sir.

MER. Death, dost thou burn me, harlot!

BAR. I beseech you, sir.

MER. Beggar, varlet, poltroon. [BEATS HIM.]

HED. Excellent, excellent!

ANA. Your French beat is the most natural beat of the world.

ASO. O that I had played at this weapon. [A CHARGE.]

PHA. Peace, now they come on; the second part.

AMO. "Madam, your beauties being so attractive, I muse you are left thus alone."

PHI. "Better be alone, sir, than ill accompanied."

AMO. "Nought can be ill, lady, that can come near your goodness."

MER. "Sweet madam, on what part of you soever a man casts his eye, he meets with perfection; you are the lively image of Venus throughout; all the graces smile in your cheeks; your beauty nourishes as well as delights; you have a tongue steeped in honey, and a breath like a panther; your breasts and forehead are whiter than goats' milk, or May blossoms; a cloud is not so soft as your skin --"

HED. Well strook, monsieur! He charges like a Frenchman indeed, thick and hotly.

MER. "Your cheeks are Cupid's baths, wherein he uses to steep himself in milk and nectar: he does light all his torches at your eyes, and instructs you how to shoot and wound with their beams. Yet I love nothing in you more than your innocence; you retain so native a simplicity, so unblamed a behaviour! Methinks, with such a love, I should find no head, nor foot of my pleasure: you are the very spirit of a lady."

ANA. Fair play, monsieur, you are too hot on the quarry; give your competitor audience.

AMO. "Lady, how stirring soever the monsieur's tongue is, he will lie by your side more dull than your eunuch."

ANA. A good stroke; that mouth was excellently put over.

AMO. "You are fair, lady --"

CRI. You offer foul, signior, to close; keep your distance; for all your bravo rampant here.

AMO. "I say you are fair, lady, let your choice be fit, as you are fair."

MER. "I say ladies do never believe they are fair, till some fool begins to doat upon them."

PHI. You play too rough, gentlemen.

AMO. "Your frenchified fool is your only fool, lady: I do yield to this honourable monsieur in all civil and humane courtesy."

[A FLOURISH.]

MER. Buz!

ANA. Admirable. Give him the prize, give him the prize: that mouth again was most courtly hit, and rare.

AMO. I knew I should pass upon him with the bitter bob.

HED. O, but the reverse was singular.

PHA. It was most subtile, Amorphus.

ASO. If I had done't, it should have been better.

MER. How heartily they applaud this, Crites!

CRI. You suffer them too long.

MER. I'll take off their edge instantly.

ANA. Name the prize, at the "Solemn Address."

PHI. Two lips wagging.

CRI. And never a wise word, I take it.

ANA. Give to Amorphus. And, upon him again; let him not draw free breath.

AMO. Thanks, fair deliverer, and my honourable judges. Madam Phantaste, you are our worthy object at this next weapon.

PHA. Most covetingly ready, Amorphus.

[SHE TAKES THE STATE INSTEAD OF PHILAUTIA.]

HED. Your monsieur is crest-fallen.

ANA. So are most of them once a year.

AMO. You will see, I shall now give him the gentle Dor presently, he forgetting to shift the colours, which are now changed with alteration of the mistress. At your last weapon, sir. "The Perfect Close." Set forward. [A CHARGE.] Intend your approach, monsieur.

MER. 'Tis yours, signior.

AMO. With your example, sir.

MER. Not I, sir.

AMO. It is your right.

MER. By no possible means.

AMO. You have the way.

MER. As I am noble --

AMO. As I am virtuous --

MER. Pardon me, sir.

AMO. I will die first.

MER. You are a tyrant in courtesy.

AMO. He is removed. -- [STAYS MERCURY ON HIS MOVING.] -- Judges, bear witness.

MER. What of that, sir?

AMO. You are removed, sir.

MER. Well.

AMO. I challenge you; you have received the Dor. Give me the prize.

MER. Soft, sir. How, the Dor?

AMO. The common mistress, you see, is changed.

MER. Right, sir.

AMO. And you have still in your hat the former colours.

MER. You lie, sir, I have none: I have pulled them out. I meant to play discoloured. [A FLOURISH.]

CRI. The Dor, the Dor, the Dor, the Dor, the Dor, the palpable Dor!

ANA. Heart of my blood, Amorphus, what have you done? stuck a disgrace upon us all, and at your last weapon!

ASO. I could have done no more.

HED. By heaven, it was most unfortunate luck.

ANA. Luck! by that candle, it was mere rashness, and oversight; would any man have ventured to play so open, and forsake his ward? D--n me, if he have not eternally undone himself in court, and discountenanced us that were his main countenance, by it.

AMO. Forgive it now: it was the solecism of my stars.

CRI. The wring by the hand, and the banquet, is ours.

MER. O, here's a lady feels like a wench of the first year; you would think her hand did melt in your touch; and the bones of her fingers ran out at length when you prest 'em, they are so gently delicate! He that had the grace to print a kiss on these lips, should taste wine and rose-leaves. O, she kisses as close as a cockle. Let's take them down, as deep as our hearts, wench, till our very souls mix. Adieu, signior: good faith I shall drink to you at supper, sir.

ANA. Stay, monsieur. Who awards you the prize?

CRI. Why, his proper merit, sir; you see he has played down your grand garb-master, here.

ANA. That's not in your logic to determine, sir: you are no courtier. This is none of your seven or nine beggarly sciences, but a certain mystery above them, wherein we that have skill must pronounce, and not such fresh men as you are.

CRI. Indeed, I must declare myself to you no profest courtling; nor to have any excellent stroke at your subtile weapons; yet if you please, I dare venture a hit with you, or your fellow, sir Dagonet, here.

ANA. With me!

CRI. Yes, sir.

ANA. Heart, I shall never have such a fortune to save myself in a fellow again, and your two reputations, gentlemen, as in this. I'll undertake him.

HED. Do, and swinge him soundly, good Anaides.

ANA. Let me alone; I'll play other manner of play, than has been seen yet. I would the prize lay on't.

MER. It shall if you will, I forgive my right.

ANA. Are you so confident! what's your weapon?

CRI. At any, I, sir.

MER. The Perfect Close, that's now the best.

ANA. Content, I'll pay your scholarity. Who offers?

CRI. Marry, that will I: I dare give you that advantage too.

ANA. You dare! well, look to your liberal sconce.

AMO. Make your play still, upon the answer, sir.

ANA. Hold your peace, you are a hobby-horse.

ASO. Sit by me, master.

MER. Now, Crites, strike home. [A CHARGE.]

CRI. You shall see me undo the assured swaggerer with a trick, instantly: I will play all his own play before him; court the wench in his garb, in his phrase, with his face; leave him not so much as a look, an eye, a stalk, or an imperfect oath, to express himself by, after me. [ASIDE TO MERCURY.]

MER. Excellent, Crites.

ANA. When begin you, sir? have you consulted?

CRI. To your cost, sir. Which is the piece stands forth to be courted? O, are you she? [TO PHILAUTIA.] "Well, madam, or sweet lady, it is so, I do love you in some sort, do you conceive? and though I am no monsieur, nor no signior, and do want, as they say, logic and sophistry, and good words, to tell you why it is so; yet by this hand and by that candle it is so: and though I be no book-worm, nor one that deals by art, to give you rhetoric and causes, why it should be so, or make it good it is so? yet, d--n me, but I know it is so, and am assured it is so, and I and my sword shall make it appear it is so, and give you reason sufficient how it can be no otherwise but so --"

HED. 'Slight, Anaides, you are mocked, and so we are all.

MER. How now, signior! what, suffer yourself to be cozened of your courtship before your face?

HED. This is plain confederacy to disgrace us: let's be gone, and plot some revenge.

AMO. "When men disgraces share,
The lesser is the care."

CRI. Nay, stay, my dear Ambition, [TO HEDON.] I can do you over too. You that tell your mistress, her beauty is all composed of theft; her hair stole from Apollo's goldy-locks; her white and red, lilies and roses stolen out of paradise; her eyes two stars, pluck'd from the sky; her nose the gnomon of Love's dial, that tells you how the clock of your heart goes: and for her other parts, as you cannot reckon them, they are so many; so you cannot recount them, they are so manifest. Yours, if his own, unfortunate Hoyden, instead of Hedon. [A FLOURISH.]

ASO. Sister, come away, I cannot endure them longer.

[EXEUNT ALL BUT MERCURY AND CRITES.]

MER. Go, Dors, and you, my madam Courting-stocks,
Follow your scorned and derided mates;
Tell to your guilty breasts, what mere gilt blocks
You are, and how unworthy human states.

CRI. Now, sacred God of Wit, if you can make
Those, whom our sports tax in these apish graces,

Kiss, like the fighting snakes, your peaceful rod,
These times shall canonise you for a god.

MER. Why, Crites, think you any noble spirit,
Or any, worth the title of a man,
Will be incensed to see the enchanted veils
Of self-conceit, and servile flattery,
Wrapt in so many folds by time and custom,
Drawn from his wronged and bewitched eyes?
Who sees not now their shape and nakedness,
Is blinder than the son of earth, the mole;
Crown'd with no more humanity, nor soul.

CRI. Though they may see it, yet the huge estate
Fancy, and form, and sensual pride have gotten,
Will make them blush for anger, not for shame,
And turn shewn nakedness to impudence.
Humour is now the test we try things in:
All power is just: nought that delights is sin.
And yet the zeal of every knowing man
Opprest with hills of tyranny, cast on virtue
By the light fancies of fools, thus transported.
Cannot but vent the Aetna of his fires,
T'inflame best bosoms with much worthier love
Than of these outward and effeminate shades;
That these vain joys, in which their wills consume
Such powers of wit and soul as are of force
To raise their beings to eternity,
May be converted on works fitting men:
And, for the practice of a forced look,
An antic gesture, or a fustian phrase,
Study the native frame of a true heart,
An inward comeliness of bounty, knowledge,

And spirit that may conform them actually
To God's high figures, which they have in power;
Which to neglect for a self-loving neatness,
Is sacrilege of an unpardon'd greatness.

MER. Then let the truth of these things strengthen thee,
In thy exempt and only man-like course;
Like it the more, the less it is respected:
Though men fail, virtue is by gods protected. --
See, here comes Arete; I'll withdraw myself. [EXIT.]

ENTER ARETE.

ARE. Crites, you must provide straight for a masque,
'Tis Cynthia's pleasure.

CRI. How, bright Arete!
Why, 'twere a labour more for Hercules:
Better and sooner durst I undertake
To make the different seasons of the year,
The winds, or elements, to sympathise,
Than their unmeasurable vanity
Dance truly in a measure. They agree!
What though all concord's born of contraries;
So many follies will confusion prove,
And like a sort of jarring instruments,
All out of tune; because, indeed, we see
There is not that analogy 'twixt discords,
As between things but merely opposite.

ARE. There is your error: for as Hermes' wand
Charms the disorders of tumultuous ghosts;
And as the strife of Chaos then did cease,

When better light than Nature's did arrive:
So, what could never in itself agree,
Forgetteth the eccentric property,
And at her sight turns forth with regular,
Whose sceptre guides the flowing ocean:
And though it did not, yet the most of them
Being either courtiers, or not wholly rude,
Respect of majesty, the place, and presence,
Will keep them within ring; especially
When they are not presented as themselves,
But masqued like others: for, in troth, not so
To incorporate them, could be nothing else,
Than like a state ungovern'd, without laws;
Or body made of nothing but diseases:
The one, through impotency, poor and wretched;
The other, for the anarchy, absurd.

CRI. But, lady, for the revellers themselves,
It would be better, in my poor conceit,
That others were employ'd; for such as are
Unfit to be in Cynthia's court, can seem
No less unfit to be in Cynthia's sports.

ARE. That, Crites, is not purposed without
Particular knowledge of the goddess' mind;
Who holding true intelligence, what follies
Had crept into her palace, she resolved
Of sports and triumphs; under that pretext,
To have them muster in their pomp and fulness,
That so she might more strictly, and to root,
Effect the reformation she intends.

CRI. I now conceive her heavenly drift in all;

And will apply my spirits to serve her will.
O thou, the very power by which I am,
And but for which it were in vain to be,
Chief next Diana, virgin heavenly fair,
Admired Arete, of them admired
Whose souls are not enkindled by the sense,
Disdain not my chaste fire, but feed the flame
Devoted truly to thy gracious name.

ARE. Leave to suspect us: Crites well shall find,
As we are now most dear, we'll prove most kind.

[WITHIN.] Arete!

ARE. Hark, I am call'd. [EXIT.]

CRI. I follow instantly.
Phoebus Apollo, if with ancient rites,
And due devotions, I have ever hung
Elaborate Paeans on thy golden shrine,
Or sung thy triumphs in a lofty strain,
Fit for a theatre of gods to hear:
And thou, the other son of mighty Jove,
Cyllenian Mercury, sweet Maia's joy,
If in the busy tumults of the mind
My path thou ever hast illumined,
For which thine altars I have oft perfumed,
And deck'd thy statues with discolour'd flowers:
Now thrive invention in this glorious court,
That not of bounty only, but of right,
Cynthia may grace, and give it life by sight. [EXIT.]

SCENE III.

ENTER HESPERUS, CYNTHIA, ARETE, TIME, PHRONESIS, AND THAUMA.

MUSIC ACCOMPANIED. HESPERUS SINGS.

Queen and huntress, chaste and fair,
Now the sun is laid to sleep,
Seated in thy silver chair,
State in wonted manner keep:
Hesperus entreats thy light,
Goddess, excellently bright.

Earth, let not thy envious shade
Dare itself to interpose;
Cynthia's shining orb was made
Heav'n to clear, when day did close:
Bless us then with wished sight,
Goddess excellently bright.

Lay thy bow of pearl apart,
And thy crystal shining quiver;
Give unto the flying hart
Space to breathe, how short soever:
Thou, that mak'st a day of night,
Goddess excellently bright.

CYN. When hath Diana, like an envious wretch,
That glitters only to his soothed self,
Denying to the world the precious use
Of hoarded wealth, withheld her friendly aid?
Monthly we spend our still-repaired shine,
And not forbid our virgin-waxen torch

To burn and blaze, while nutriment doth last:
That once consumed, out of Jove's treasury
A new we take, and stick it in our sphere,
To give the mutinous kind of wanting men
Their look'd-for light. Yet what is their desert?
Bounty is wrong'd, interpreted as due;
Mortals can challenge not a ray, by right,
Yet do expect the whole of Cynthia's light.
But if that deities withdrew their gifts
For human follies, what could men deserve
But death and darkness? It behoves the high,
For their own sakes, to do things worthily.

ARE. Most true, most sacred goddess; for the heavens
Receive no good of all the good they do:
Nor Jove, nor you, nor other heavenly Powers,
Are fed with fumes, which do from incense rise,
Or sacrifices reeking in their gore;
Yet, for the care which you of mortals have,
(Whose proper good it is that they be so;)
You well are pleased with odours redolent:
But ignorant is all the race of men,
Which still complains, not knowing why, or when.

CYN. Else, noble Arete, they would not blame,
And tax, or for unjust, or for as proud,
Thy Cynthia, in the things which are indeed
The greatest glories in our starry crown;
Such is our chastity, which safely scorns,
Not love, for who more fervently doth love
Immortal honour, and divine renown?
But giddy Cupid, Venus' frantic son.
Yet, Arete, if by this veiled light

We but discover'd (what we not discern)
Any the least of imputations stand
Ready to sprinkle our unspotted fame
With note of lightness, from these revels near:
Not, for the empire of the universe,
Should night, or court, this whatsoever shine,
Or grace of ours, unhappily enjoy.
Place and occasion are two privy thieves;
And from poor innocent ladies often steal
The best of things, an honourable name;
To stay with follies, or where faults may be,
Infers a crime, although the party free.

ARE. How Cynthianly, that is, how worthily
And like herself, the matchless Cynthia speaks!
Infinite jealousies, infinite regards,
Do watch about the true virginity:
But Phoebe lives from all, not only fault,
But as from thought, so from suspicion free.
Thy presence broad-seals our delights for pure;
What's done in Cynthia's sight, is done secure.

CYN. That then so answer'd, dearest Arete,
What th' argument, or of what sort our sports
Are like to be this night, I not demand.
Nothing which duty, and desire to please,
Bears written in the forehead, comes amiss.
But unto whose invention must we owe
The complement of this night's furniture?

ARE. Excellent goddess, to a man's, whose worth,
Without hyperbole, I thus may praise;
One at least studious of deserving well,

And, to speak truth, indeed deserving well.
Potential merit stands for actual,
Where only opportunity doth want,
Not will, nor power; both which in him abound,
One whom the Muses and Minerva love;
For whom should they, than Crites, more esteem,
Whom Phoebus, though not Fortune, holdeth dear?
And, which convinceth excellence in him,
A principal admirer of yourself:
Even through the ungentle injuries of Fate,
And difficulties, which do virtue choke,
Thus much of him appears. What other things
Of farther note do lie unborn in him,
Them I do leave for cherishment to shew,
And for a goddess graciously to judge.

CYN. We have already judged him, Arete,
Nor are we ignorant how noble minds
Suffer too much through those indignities
Which times and vicious persons cast on them.
Ourself have ever vowed to esteem
As virtue for itself, so fortune, base;
Who's first in worth, the same be first in place.
Nor farther notice, Arete, we crave
Then thine approval's sovereign warranty:
Let 't be thy care to make us known to him;
Cynthia shall brighten what the world made dim.

[EXIT ARETE.]

THE FIRST MASQUE.

ENTER CUPID, DISGUISED AS ANTEROS, FOLLOWED BY STORGE, AGLAIA, EUPHANTASTE,
AND APHELEIA.

CUP. Clear pearl of heaven, and, not to be farther ambitious in titles, Cynthia! the fame of this illustrious night, among others, hath also drawn these four fair virgins from the palace of their queen Perfection, (a word which makes no sufficient difference betwixt her's and thine,) to visit thy imperial court: for she, their sovereign, not finding where to dwell among men, before her return to heaven, advised them wholly to consecrate themselves to thy celestial service, as in whose clear spirit (the proper element and sphere of virtue) they should behold not her alone, their ever-honoured mistress, but themselves (more truly themselves) to live enthronised. Herself would have commended them unto thy favour more particularly, but that she knows no commendation is more available with thee, than that of proper virtue. Nevertheless she willed them to present this crystal mound, a note of monarchy, and symbol of perfection, to thy more worthy deity; which, as here by me they most humbly do, so amongst the rarities thereof, that is the chief, to shew whatsoever the world hath excellent, howsoever remote and various. But your irradiate judgment will soon discover the secrets of this little crystal world. Themselves, to appear more plainly, because they know nothing more odious then false pretexts, have chosen to express their several qualities thus in several colours.

The first, in citron colour, is natural affection, which, given us to procure our good, is sometime called Storge; and as every one is nearest to himself, so this handmaid of reason, allowable Self-love, as it is without harm, so are none without it: her place in the court of Perfection was to quicken minds in the pursuit of honour. Her device is a perpendicular level, upon a cube or square; the word, "se suo modulo"; alluding to that true measure of one's self, which as every one ought to make, so is it most conspicuous in thy divine example.

The second, in green is Aglaia, delectable and pleasant conversation, whose property it is to move a kindly delight, and sometime not without laughter: her office to entertain assemblies, and keep societies together with fair familiarity. Her device, within a ring of clouds, a heart with shine about it; the word, 'curarum nubila pello': an allegory of Cynthia's light, which no less clears the sky then her fair mirth the heart.

The third, in the discoloured mantle spangled all over, is Euphantaste, a well-conceited Wittiness, and employed in honouring the court with the riches of her pure invention. Her device, upon a Petasus, or Mercurial hat, a crescent; The word; "sic laus ingenii"; inferring that the praise and glory of wit doth ever increase, as doth thy growing moon.

The fourth, in white, is Apheleia, a nymph as pure and simple as the soul, or as an abrase table, and is therefore called Simplicity; without folds, without plaits, without colour, without counterfeit; and (to speak plainly) plainness itself. Her device is no device. The word under her silver shield, "omnis abest fucus"; alluding to thy spotless self, who art as far from impurity as from mortality.

Myself, celestial goddess, more fit for the court of Cynthia than the arbours of Cytherea, am called Anteros, or Love's enemy; the more welcome therefore to thy court, and the fitter to conduct this quaternion, who, as they are thy professed votaries, and for that cause adversaries to Love, yet thee, perpetual virgin, they both love, and vow to love eternally.

RE-ENTER ARETE, WITH CRITES.

CYN. Not without wonder, nor without delight
Mine eyes have view'd, in contemplation's depth,
This work of wit, divine and excellent:
What shape, what substance, or what unknown power,
In virgin's habit, crown'd with laurel leaves,
And olive-branches woven in between,
On sea-girt rocks, like to a goddess shines!
O front! O face! O all celestial, sure,
And more than mortal! Arete, behold
Another Cynthia, and another queen,
Whose glory, like a lasting plenilune,
Seems ignorant of what it is to wane.
Nor under heaven an object could be found
More fit to please. Let Crites make approach.
Bounty forbids to pall our thanks with stay,
Or to defer our favour, after view:
The time of grace is, when the cause is new.

ARE. Lo, here the man, celestial Delia,
Who (like a circle bounded in itself)
Contains as much as man in fulness may.
Lo, here the man; who not of usual earth,
But of that nobler and more precious mould
Which Phoebus' self doth temper, is composed;
And who, though all were wanting to reward,
Yet to himself he would not wanting be:
Thy favours gain is his ambition's most,

And labour's best; who (humble in his height)
Stands fixed silent in thy glorious sight.

CYN. With no less pleasure than we have beheld
This precious crystal work of rarest wit,
Our eye doth read thee, now instiled, our Crites;
Whom learning, virtue, and our favour last,
Exempteth from the gloomy multitude.
With common eye the Supreme should not see:
Henceforth be ours, the more thyself to be.

CRI. Heaven's purest light, whose orb may be eclipsed,
But not thy praise; divinest Cynthia!
How much too narrow for so high a grace,
Thine (save therein) the most unworthy Crites
Doth find himself! for ever shine thy fame;
Thine honours ever, as thy beauties do.
In me they must, my dark world's chiefest lights,
By whose propitious beams my powers are raised
To hope some part of those most lofty points,
Which blessed Arete hath pleased to name,
As marks, to which my endeavour's steps should bend:
Mine, as begun at thee, in thee must end.

THE SECOND MASQUE.

ENTER MERCURY AS A PAGE, INTRODUCING EUCOSMOS, EUPATHES, EUTOLMOS, AND EUCOLOS.

MER. Sister of Phoebus, to whose bright orb we owe, that we not complain of his absence; these four brethren (for they are brethren, and sons of Eutaxia, a lady known, and highly beloved of your resplendent deity) not able to be absent, when Cynthia held a solemnity, officiously insinuate themselves into thy presence: for, as there are four cardinal virtues, upon which the whole frame of the court doth move, so are these the four cardinal properties, without which the body of compliment moveth not. With these four silver javelins, (which they bear in their hands) they support in princes' courts the state of the presence, as by office they are obliged: which, though here they may seem superfluous, yet, for honour's sake, they thus presume to visit thee, having also been employed in the palace of queen Perfection. And though to them that would make themselves gracious to a goddess, sacrifices were fitter than presents, or impresses, yet they both hope thy favour, and (in place of either) use several symbols, containing the titles of thy imperial dignity.

First, the hithermost, in the changeable blue and green robe, is the commendably-fashioned gallant Eucosmos; whose courtly habit is the grace of the presence, and delight of the surveying eye; whom ladies understand by the names of Neat and Elegant. His symbol is, "divae virgini," in which he would express thy deity's principal glory, which hath ever been virginity.

The second, in the rich accoutrement, and robe of purple, empaled with gold, is Eupathes; who entertains his mind with an harmless, but not incurious variety; all the objects of his senses are sumptuous, himself a gallant, that, without excess, can make use of superfluity, go richly in embroideries, jewels, and what not, without vanity, and fare delicately without gluttony; and therefore (not without cause) is universally thought to be of fine humour. His symbol is, "divae optimae"; an attribute to express thy goodness, in which thou so resemblest Jove thy father.

The third, in the blush-coloured suit, is Eutolmos, as duly

respecting others, as never neglecting himself; commonly known by the title of good Audacity; to courts and courtly assemblies a guest most acceptable. His symbol is, "divae viragini"; to express thy hardy courage in chase of savage beasts, which harbour in woods and wildernesses.

The fourth, in watchet tinsel, is the kind and truly benefique Eucolos, who imparteth not without respect, but yet without difficulty, and hath the happiness to make every kindness seem double, by the timely and freely bestowing thereof. He is the chief of them, who by the vulgar are said to be of good nature. His symbol is, "divae maximae"; an adjunct to signify thy greatness, which in heaven, earth, and hell, is formidable.

MUSIC. A DANCE BY THE TWO MASQUES JOINED, DURING WHICH CUPID AND
MERCURY RETIRE TO THE SIDE OF THE STAGE.

CUP. Is not that Amorphus, the traveller?

MER. As though it were not! do you not see how his legs are in travail with a measure?

CUP. Hedon, thy master is next.

MER. What, will Cupid turn nomenclator, and cry them?

CUP. No, faith, but I have a comedy toward, that would not be lost for a kingdom.

MER. In good time, for Cupid will prove the comedy.

CUP. Mercury, I am studying how to match them.

MER. How to mismatch them were harder.

CUP. They are the nymphs must do it; I shall sport myself with their passions above measure.

MER. Those nymphs would be tamed a little indeed, but I fear thou has not arrows for the purpose.

CUP. O yes, here be of all sorts, flights, rovers, and butt-shafts. But I can wound with a brandish, and never draw bow for the matter.

MER. I cannot but believe it, my invisible archer, and yet methinks you are tedious.

CUP. It behoves me to be somewhat circumspect, Mercury; for if Cynthia hear the twang of my bow, she'll go near to whip me with the string; therefore, to prevent that, I thus discharge a brandish upon -- it makes no matter which of the couples. Phantaste and Amorphus, at you. [WAVES HIS ARROW AT THEM.]

MER. Will the shaking of a shaft strike them into such a fever of affection?

CUP. As well as the wink of an eye: but, I pray thee, hinder me not with thy prattle.

MER. Jove forbid I hinder thee; Marry, all that I fear is Cynthia's presence, which, with the cold of her chastity, casteth such an antiperistasis about the place, that no heat of thine will tarry with the patient.

CUP. It will tarry the rather, for the antiperistasis will keep it in.

MER. I long to see the experiment.

CUP. Why, their marrow boils already, or they are all turn'd eunuchs.

MER. Nay, an't be so, I'll give over speaking, and be a spectator only.

[THE FIRST DANCE ENDS.]

AMO. Cynthia, by my bright soul, is a right exquisite and spendidious lady; yet Amorphus, I think, hath seen more fashions, I am sure more countries; but whether I have or not, what need we gaze on Cynthia, that have ourself to admire?

PHA. O, excellent Cynthia! yet if Phantaste sat where she does, and had such attire on her head, (for attire can do much,) I say no more -- but goddesses are goddesses, and Phantaste is as she is! I would the revels were done once, I might go to my school of glass again, and learn to do myself right after all this ruffling.

[MUSIC; THEY BEGIN THE SECOND DANCE.]

MER. How now Cupid? here's a wonderful change with your brandish! do you not hear how they dote?

CUP. What prodigy is this? no word of love, no mention, no motion!

MER. Not a word my little ignis fatue, not a word.

CUP. Are my darts enchanted? is their vigour gone? is their virtue --

MER. What! Cupid turned jealous of himself? ha, ha, ha!

CUP. Laughs Mercury?

MER. Is Cupid angry?

CUP. Hath he not cause, when his purpose is so deluded?

MER. A rare comedy, it shall be entitled Cupid's?

CUP. Do not scorn us Hermes.

MER. Choler and Cupid are two fiery things; I scorn them not. But I see that come to pass which I presaged in the beginning.

CUP. You cannot tell: perhaps the physic will not work so soon upon some as upon others. It may be the rest are not so resty.

MER. "Ex ungue"; you know the old adage; as these so are the remainder.

CUP. I'll try: this is the same shaft with which I wounded Argurion. [WAVES HIS ARROW AGAIN.]

MER. Ay, but let me save you a labour, Cupid: there were certain bottles of water fetch'd, and drunk off since that time, by these gallants.

CUP. Jove strike me into the earth! the Fountain of Self-love!

MER. Nay faint not Cupid.

CUP. I remember'd it not.

MER. Faith, it was ominous to take the name of Anteros upon you; you know not what charm or enchantment lies in the word: you saw, I durst not venture upon any device in our presentment, but was content to be no other then a simple page. Your arrows' properties, (to keep decorum,) Cupid, are suited, it should seem, to the nature of him you personate.

CUP. Indignity not to be borne!

MER. Nay rather, an attempt to have been forborne.

[THE SECOND DANCE ENDS.]

CUP. How might I revenge myself on this insulting Mercury? there's Crites, his minion, he has not tasted of this water? [WAVES HIS ARROW AT CRITES.] It shall be so. Is Crites turn'd dotard on himself too?

MER. That follows not, because the venom of your shafts cannot pierce him, Cupid.

CUP. As though there were one antidote for these, and another for him?

MER. As though there were not; or, as if one effect might not arise of diverse causes? What say you to Cynthia, Arete, Phronesis, Time, and others there?

CUP. They are divine.

MER. And Crites aspires to be so.

[MUSIC; THEY BEGIN THE THIRD DANCE.]

CUP. But that shall not serve him.

MER. 'Tis like to do it, at this time. But Cupid is grown too covetous, that will not spare one of a multitude.

CUP. One is more than a multitude.

MER. Arete's favour makes any one shot-proof against thee, Cupid. I pray thee, light honey-bee, remember thou art not now in Adonis' garden, but in Cynthia's presence, where thorns lie in garrison about the roses. Soft, Cynthia speaks.

CYN. Ladies and gallants of our court, to end,
And give a timely period to our sports,
Let us conclude them, with declining night;
Our empire is but of the darker half.
And if you judge it any recompence
For your faire pains, t' have earn'd Diana's thanks,
Diana grants them, and bestows their crown
To gratify your acceptable zeal.
For you are they, that not, as some have done,
Do censure us, as too severe and sour,
But as, more rightly, gracious to the good;
Although we not deny, unto the proud,
Or the profane, perhaps indeed austere:
For so Actaeon, by presuming far,
Did, to our grief, incur a fatal doom;

And so, swoln Niobe, comparing more
Than he presumed, was trophaeed into stone.
But are we therefore judged too extreme?
Seems it no crime to enter sacred bowers,
And hallowed places, with impure aspect,
Most lewdly to pollute? Seems it no crime
To brave a deity? Let mortals learn
To make religion of offending heaven.
And not at all to censure powers divine.
To men this argument should stand for firm,
A goddess did it, therefore it was good:
We are not cruel, nor delight in blood. --
But what have serious repetitions
To do with revels, and the sports of court?
We not intend to sour your late delights
With harsh expostulation. Let it suffice
That we take notice, and can take revenge
Of these calumnious and lewd blasphemies.
For we are no less Cynthia than we were,
Nor is our power, but as ourself, the same:
Though we have now put on no tire of shine,
But mortal eyes undazzled may endure.
Years are beneath the spheres, and time makes weak
Things under heaven, not powers which govern heaven.
And though ourself be in ourself secure,
Yet let not mortals challenge to themselves
Immunity from thence. Lo, this is all:
Honour hath store of spleen, but wanteth gall.
Once more we cast the slumber of our thanks
On your ta'en toil, which here let take an end:
And that we not mistake your several worths,
Nor you our favour, from yourselves remove
What makes you not yourselves, those clouds of masque

Particular pains particular thanks do ask.

[THE DANCERS UNMASK.]

How! let me view you. Ha! are we contemn'd?
Is there so little awe of our disdain,
That any (under trust of their disguise)
Should mix themselves with others of the court,
And, without forehead, boldly press so far,
As farther none? How apt is lenity
To be abused! severity to be loath'd!
And yet, how much more doth the seeming face
Of neighbour virtues, and their borrow'd names,
Add of lewd boldness to loose vanities!
Who would have thought that Philautia durst
Or have usurped noble Storge's name,
Or with that theft have ventured on our eyes?
Who would have thought, that all of them should hope
So much of our connivence, as to come
To grace themselves with titles not their own?
Instead of med'cines, have we maladies?
And such imposthumes as Phantaste is
Grow in our palace? We must lance these sores,
Or all will putrify. Nor are these all,
For we suspect a farther fraud than this:
Take off our veil, that shadows many depart,
And shapes appear, beloved Arete -- So,
Another face of things presents itself,
Than did of late. What! feather'd Cupid masqued,
And masked like Anteros? And stay! more strange!
Dear Mercury, our brother, like a page,
To countenance the ambush of the boy!
Nor endeth our discovery as yet:

Gelaia, like a nymph, that, but erewhile,
In male attire, did serve Anaides? --
Cupid came hither to find sport and game,
Who heretofore hath been too conversant
Among our train, but never felt revenge:
And Mercury bare Cupid company.
Cupid, we must confess, this time of mirth,
Proclaim'd by us, gave opportunity
To thy attempts, although no privilege:
Tempt us no farther; we cannot endure
Thy presence longer; vanish hence, away!
[EXIT CUPID.]
You Mercury, we must entreat to stay,
And hear what we determine of the rest;
For in this plot we well perceive your hand.
But, (for we mean not a censorian task,
And yet to lance these ulcers grown so ripe,)
Dear Arete, and Crites, to you two
We give the charge; impose what pains you please:
Th' incurable cut off, the rest reform,
Remembering ever what we first decreed,
Since revels were proclaim'd, let now none bleed.

ARE. How well Diana can distinguish times,
And sort her censures, keeping to herself
The doom of gods, leaving the rest to us!
Come, cite them, Crites, first, and then proceed.

CRI. First, Philautia, for she was the first,
Then light Gelaia in Aglaia's name,
Thirdly, Phantaste, and Moria next,
Main Follies all, and of the female crew:
Amorphus, or Eucosmos' counterfeit,

Voluptuous Hedon ta'en for Eupathes,
Brazen Anaides, and Asotus last,
With his two pages, Morus, and Prosaites;
And thou, the traveller's evil, Cos, approach,
Impostors all, and male deformities --

ARE. Nay, forward, for I delegate my power.
And will that at thy mercy they do stand,
Whom they so oft, so plainly scorn'd before.
'Tis virtue which they want, and wanting it,
Honour no garment to their backs can fit.
Then, Crites, practise thy discretion.

CRI. Adored Cynthia, and bright Arete,
Another might seem fitter for this task,
Than Crites far, but that you judge not so:
For I (not to appear vindicative,
Or mindful of contempts, which I contemn'd,
As done of impotence) must be remiss:
Who, as I was the author, in some sort,
To work their knowledge into Cynthia's sight,
So should be much severer to revenge
The indignity hence issuing to her name:
But there's not one of these who are unpain'd,
Or by themselves unpunished; for vice
Is like a fury to the vicious mind,
And turns delight itself to punishment.
But we must forward, to define their doom.
You are offenders, that must be confess'd;
Do you confess it?

ALL. We do.

CRI. And that you merit sharp correction?

ALL. Yes.

CRI. Then we (reserving unto Delia's grace
Her farther pleasure, and to Arete
What Delia granteth) thus do sentence you:
That from this place (for penance known of all,
Since you have drunk so deeply of Self-love)
You, two and two, singing a Palinode,
March to your several homes by Niobe's stone,
And offer up two tears a-piece thereon,
That it may change the name, as you must change,
And of a stone be called Weeping-cross:
Because it standeth cross of Cynthia's way,
One of whose names is sacred Trivia.
And after penance thus perform'd you pass
In like set order, not as Midas did,
To wash his gold off into Tagus' stream;
  But to the Well of knowledge, Helicon;
Where, purged of your present maladies,
Which are not few, nor slender, you become
Such as you fain would seem, and then return,
Offering your service to great Cynthia.
This is your sentence, if the goddess please
To ratify it with her high consent;
The scope of wise mirth unto fruit is bent.

CYN. We do approve thy censure belov'd Crites;
Which Mercury, thy true propitious friend,
(A deity next Jove beloved of us,)
Will undertake to see exactly done.
And for this service of discovery,

Perform'd by thee, in honour of our name,
We vow to guerdon it with such due grace
As shall become our bounty, and thy place.
Princes that would their people should do well,
Must at themselves begin, as at the head;
For men, by their example, pattern out
Their imitations, and regard of laws:
A virtuous court, a world to virtue draws.

[EXEUNT CYNTHIA AND HER NYMPHS, FOLLOWED BY ARETE AND CRITES: --
AMORPHUS, PHANTASTE, ETC., GO OFF THE STAGE IN PAIRS, SINGING THE
FOLLOWING]

PALINODE.

AMO. From Spanish shrugs, French faces, smirks, irpes, and all affected humours,

CHORUS. Good Mercury defend us.

PHA. From secret friends, sweet servants, loves, doves, and such fantastic humours,

CHORUS. Good Mercury defend us.

AMO. From stabbing of arms, flap-dragons, healths, whiffs, and all such swaggering humours,

CHORUS. Good Mercury defend us.

PHA. From waving fans, coy glances, glicks, cringes, and all such simpering humours,

CHORUS. Good Mercury defend us.

AMO. From making love by attorney, courting of puppets, and paying for new acquaintance.

CHORUS. Good Mercury defend us.

PHA. From perfumed dogs, monkies, sparrows, dildoes, and paraquettoes,

CHORUS. Good Mercury defend us.

AMO. From wearing bracelets of hair, shoe-ties, gloves, garters, and rings with poesies.

CHORUS. Good Mercury defend us.

PHA. From pargetting, painting, slicking, glazing, and renewing old rivelled faces.

CHORUS. Good Mercury defend us.

AMO. From 'squiring to tilt yards, play-houses, pageants, and all such public places.

CHORUS. Good Mercury defend us.

PHA. From entertaining one gallant to gull another, and making fools of either,

CHORUS. Good Mercury defend us.

AMO. From belying ladies' favours, noblemen's countenance, coining counterfeit employments, vain-glorious taking to them other men's services, and all self-loving humours,

CHORUS. Good Mercury defend us.

MERCURY AND CRITES SING.

Now each one dry his weeping eyes,
And to the Well of Knowledge haste;
Where, purged of your maladies,
You may of sweeter waters taste:
And, with refined voice, report
The grace of Cynthia, and her court.

[EXEUNT.

THE EPILOGUE.

Gentles, be't known to you, since I went in
I am turn'd rhymer, and do thus begin.
The author (jealous how your sense doth take
His travails) hath enjoined me to make
Some short and ceremonious epilogue;
But if I yet know what, I am a rogue:
He ties me to such laws as quite distract
My thoughts, and would a year of time exact.
I neither must be faint, remiss, nor sorry,
Sour, serious, confident, nor peremptory:
But betwixt these. Let's see; to lay the blame
Upon the children's action, that were lame.

To crave your favour, with a begging knee,
Were to distrust the writer's faculty.
To promise better at the next we bring,
Prorogues disgrace, commends not any thing.
Stiffly to stand on this, and proudly approve
The play, might tax the maker of Self-love.
I'll only speak what I have heard him say,
"By -- 'tis good, and if you like't, you may."

"Ecce rubet quidam, pallet, stupet, oscitat, odit
Hoc volo: nunc nobis carmina nostra placent.

GLOSSARY

ABATE, cast down, subdue.

ABHORRING, repugnant (to), at variance.

ABJECT, base, degraded thing, outcast.

ABRASE, smooth, blank.

ABSOLUTE(LY), faultless(ly).

ABSTRACTED, abstract, abstruse.

ABUSE, deceive, insult, dishonour, make ill use of.

ACATER, caterer.

ACATES, cates.

ACCEPTIVE, willing, ready to accept, receive.

ACCOMMODATE, fit, befitting. (The word was a fashionable one and used on all occasions. See "Henry IV.," pt. 2, iii. 4).

ACCOST, draw near, approach.

ACKNOWN, confessedly acquainted with.

ACME, full maturity.

ADALANTADO, lord deputy or governor of a Spanish province.

ADJECTION, addition.

ADMIRATION, astonishment.

ADMIRE, wonder, wonder at.

ADROP, philosopher's stone, or substance from which obtained.

ADSCRIVE, subscribe.

ADULTERATE, spurious, counterfeit.

ADVANCE, lift.

ADVERTISE, inform, give intelligence.

ADVERTISED, "be --," be it known to you.

ADVERTISEMENT, intelligence.

ADVISE, consider, bethink oneself, deliberate.

ADVISED, informed, aware; "are you --?" have you found that out?

AFFECT, love, like; aim at; move.

AFFECTED, disposed; beloved.

AFFECTIONATE, obstinate; prejudiced.

AFFECTS, affections.

AFFRONT, "give the -- ," face.

AFFY, have confidence in; betroth.

AFTER, after the manner of.

AGAIN, AGAINST, in anticipation of.

AGGRAVATE, increase, magnify, enlarge upon.

AGNOMINATION. See Paranomasie.

AIERY, nest, brood.

AIM, guess.

ALL HID, children's cry at hide-and-seek.

ALL-TO, completely, entirely ("all-to-be-laden").

ALLOWANCE, approbation, recognition.

ALMA-CANTARAS (astronomy), parallels of altitude.

ALMAIN, name of a dance.

ALMUTEN, planet of chief influence in the horoscope.

ALONE, unequalled, without peer.

ALUDELS, subliming pots.

AMAZED, confused, perplexed.

AMBER, AMBRE, ambergris.

AMBREE, MARY, a woman noted for her valour at the siege of Ghent, 1458.

AMES-ACE, lowest throw at dice.

AMPHIBOLIES, ambiguities.

AMUSED, bewildered, amazed.

AN, if.

ANATOMY, skeleton, or dissected body.

ANDIRONS, fire-dogs.

ANGEL, gold coin worth 10 shillings, stamped with the figure of the archangel Michael.

ANNESH CLEARE, spring known as Agnes le Clare.

ANSWER, return hit in fencing.

ANTIC, ANTIQUE, clown, buffoon.

ANTIC, like a buffoon.

ANTIPERISTASIS, an opposition which enhances the quality it opposes.

APOZEM, decoction.

APPERIL, peril.

APPLE-JOHN, APPLE-SQUIRE, pimp, pander.

APPLY, attach.

APPREHEND, take into custody.

APPREHENSIVE, quick of perception; able to perceive and appreciate.

APPROVE, prove, confirm.

APT, suit, adapt; train, prepare; dispose, incline.

APT(LY), suitable(y), opportune(ly).

APTITUDE, suitableness.

ARBOR, "make the --," cut up the game (Gifford).

ARCHES, Court of Arches.

ARCHIE, Archibald Armstrong, jester to James I. and Charles I.

ARGAILE, argol, crust or sediment in wine casks.

ARGENT-VIVE, quicksilver.

ARGUMENT, plot of a drama; theme, subject; matter in question; token, proof.

ARRIDE, please.

ARSEDINE, mixture of copper and zinc, used as an imitation of gold-leaf.

ARTHUR, PRINCE, reference to an archery show by a society who assumed arms, etc., of Arthur's knights.

ARTICLE, item.

ARTIFICIALLY, artfully.

ASCENSION, evaporation, distillation.

ASPIRE, try to reach, obtain, long for.

ASSALTO (Italian), assault.

ASSAY, draw a knife along the belly of the deer, a

ceremony of the hunting-field.

ASSOIL, solve.

ASSURE, secure possession or reversion of.

ATHANOR, a digesting furnace, calculated to keep up a constant heat.

ATONE, reconcile.

ATTACH, attack, seize.

AUDACIOUS, having spirit and confidence.

AUTHENTIC(AL), of authority, authorised, trustworthy, genuine.

AVISEMENT, reflection, consideration.

AVOID, begone! get rid of.

AWAY WITH, endure.

AZOCH, Mercurius Philosophorum.

BABION, baboon.

BABY, doll.

BACK-SIDE, back premises.

BAFFLE, treat with contempt.

BAGATINE, Italian coin, worth about the third of a farthing.

BAIARD, horse of magic powers known to old romance.

BALDRICK, belt worn across the breast to support bugle, etc.

BALE (of dice), pair.

BALK, overlook, pass by, avoid.

BALLACE, ballast.

BALLOO, game at ball.

BALNEUM (BAIN MARIE), a vessel for holding hot water in which other vessels are stood for heating.

BANBURY, "brother of --," Puritan.

BANDOG, dog tied or chained up.

BANE, woe, ruin.

BANQUET, a light repast; dessert.

BARB, to clip gold.

BARBEL, fresh-water fish.

BARE, meer; bareheaded; it was "a particular mark of state and grandeur for the coachman to be uncovered" (Gifford).

BARLEY-BREAK, game somewhat similar to base.

BASE, game of prisoner's base.

BASES, richly embroidered skirt reaching to the knees, or lower.

BASILISK, fabulous reptile, believed to slay with its eye.

BASKET, used for the broken provision collected for prisoners.

BASON, basons, etc., were beaten by the attendant mob when bad characters were "carted."

BATE, be reduced; abate, reduce.

BATOON, baton, stick.

BATTEN, feed, grow fat.

BAWSON, badger.

BEADSMAN, prayer-man, one engaged to pray for another.

BEAGLE, small hound; fig. spy.

BEAR IN HAND, keep in suspense, deceive with false hopes.

BEARWARD, bear leader.

BEDPHERE. See Phere.

BEDSTAFF, (?) wooden pin in the side of the bedstead for supporting the bedclothes (Johnson); one of the sticks or "laths"; a stick used in making a bed.

BEETLE, heavy mallet.

BEG, "I'd -- him," the custody of minors and idiots was begged for; likewise property fallen forfeit to the Crown ("your house had been begged").

BELL-MAN, night watchman.

BENJAMIN, an aromatic gum.

BERLINA, pillory.

BESCUMBER, defile.

BESLAVE, beslabber.

BESOGNO, beggar.

BESPAWLE, bespatter.

BETHLEHEM GABOR, Transylvanian hero, proclaimed King of Hungary.

BEVER, drinking.

BEVIS, SIR, knight of romance whose horse was equally celebrated.

BEWRAY, reveal, make known.

BEZANT, heraldic term: small gold circle.

BEZOAR'S STONE, a remedy known by this name was a

supposed antidote to poison.

BID-STAND, highwayman.

BIGGIN, cap, similar to that worn by the Beguines; nightcap.

BILIVE (belive), with haste.

BILK, nothing, empty talk.

BILL, kind of pike.

BILLET, wood cut for fuel, stick.

BIRDING, thieving.

BLACK SANCTUS, burlesque hymn, any unholy riot.

BLANK, originally a small French coin.

BLANK, white.

BLANKET, toss in a blanket.

BLAZE, outburst of violence.

BLAZE, (her.) blazon; publish abroad.

BLAZON, armorial bearings; fig. all that pertains to good birth and breeding.

BLIN, "withouten --," without ceasing.

BLOW, puff up.

BLUE, colour of servants' livery, hence "-- order," "-- waiters".

BLUSHET, blushing one.

BOB, jest, taunt.

BOB, beat, thump.

BODGE, measure.

BODKIN, dagger, or other short, pointed weapon; long pin with which the women fastened up their hair.

BOLT, roll (of material).

BOLT, dislodge, rout out; sift (boulting-tub).

BOLT'S-HEAD, long, straight-necked vessel for distillation.

BOMBARD SLOPS, padded, puffed-out breeches.

BONA ROBA, "good, wholesome, plum-cheeked wench" (Johnson) -- not always used in compliment.

BONNY-CLABBER, sour butter-milk.

BOOKHOLDER, prompter.

BOOT, "to --," into the bargain; "no --," of no avail.

BORACHIO, bottle made of skin.

BORDELLO, brothel.

BORNE IT, conducted, carried it through.

BOTTLE (of hay), bundle, truss.

BOTTOM, skein or ball of thread; vessel.

BOURD, jest.

BOVOLI, snails or cockles dressed in the Italian manner (Gifford).

BOW-POT, flower vase or pot.

BOYS, "terrible --," "angry --," roystering young bucks. (See Nares).

BRABBLES (BRABBLESH), brawls.

BRACH, bitch.

BRADAMANTE, a heroine in "Orlando Furioso."

BRADLEY, ARTHUR OF, a lively character commemorated in ballads.

BRAKE, frame for confining a horse's feet while being shod, or strong curb or bridle; trap.

BRANCHED, with "detached sleeve ornaments, projecting

from the shoulders of the gown" (Gifford).

BRANDISH, flourish of weapon.

BRASH, brace.

BRAVE, bravado, braggart speech.

BRAVE (adv.), gaily, finely (apparelled).

BRAVERIES, gallants.

BRAVERY, extravagant gaiety of apparel.

BRAVO, bravado, swaggerer.

BRAZEN-HEAD, speaking head made by Roger Bacon.

BREATHE, pause for relaxation; exercise.

BREATH UPON, speak dispraisingly of.

BREND, burn.

BRIDE-ALE, wedding feast.

BRIEF, abstract; (mus.) breve.

BRISK, smartly dressed.

BRIZE, breese, gadfly.

BROAD-SEAL, state seal.

BROCK, badger (term of contempt).

BROKE, transact business as a broker.

BROOK, endure, put up with.

BROUGHTON, HUGH, an English divine and Hebrew scholar.

BRUIT, rumour.

BUCK, wash.

BUCKLE, bend.

BUFF, leather made of buffalo skin, used for military and serjeants' coats, etc.

BUFO, black tincture.

BUGLE, long-shaped bead.

BULLED, (?) bolled, swelled.

BULLIONS, trunk hose.

BULLY, term of familiar endearment.

BUNGY, Friar Bungay, who had a familiar in the shape of a dog.

BURDEN, refrain, chorus.

BURGONET, closely-fitting helmet with visor.

BURGULLION, braggadocio.

BURN, mark wooden measures ("--ing of cans").

BURROUGH, pledge, security.

BUSKIN, half-boot, foot gear reaching high up the leg.

BUTT-SHAFT, barbless arrow for shooting at butts.

BUTTER, NATHANIEL ("Staple of News"), a compiler of general news. (See Cunningham).

BUTTERY-HATCH, half-door shutting off the buttery, where provisions and liquors were stored.

BUY, "he bought me," formerly the guardianship of wards could be bought.

BUZ, exclamation to enjoin silence.

BUZZARD, simpleton.

BY AND BY, at once.

BY(E), "on the ," incidentally, as of minor or secondary importance; at the side.

BY-CHOP, by-blow, bastard.

CADUCEUS, Mercury's wand.

CALIVER, light kind of musket.

CALLET, woman of ill repute.

CALLOT, coif worn on the wigs of our judges or serjeants-at-law (Gifford).

CALVERED, crimped, or sliced and pickled. (See Nares).

CAMOUCCIO, wretch, knave.

CAMUSED, flat.

CAN, knows.

CANDLE-RENT, rent from house property.

CANDLE-WASTER, one who studies late.

CANTER, sturdy beggar.

CAP OF MAINTENCE, an insignia of dignity, a cap of state borne before kings at their coronation; also an heraldic term.

CAPABLE, able to comprehend, fit to receive instruction, impression.

CAPANEUS, one of the "Seven against Thebes."

CARACT, carat, unit of weight for precious stones, etc.; value, worth.

CARANZA, Spanish author of a book on duelling.

CARCANET, jewelled ornament for the neck.

CARE, take care; object.

CAROSH, coach, carriage.

CARPET, table-cover.

CARRIAGE, bearing, behaviour.

CARWHITCHET, quip, pun.

CASAMATE, casemate, fortress.

CASE, a pair.

CASE, "in --," in condition.

CASSOCK, soldier's loose overcoat.

CAST, flight of hawks, couple.

CAST, throw dice; vomit; forecast, calculate.

CAST, cashiered.

CASTING-GLASS, bottle for sprinkling perfume.

CASTRIL, kestrel, falcon.

CAT, structure used in sieges.

CATAMITE, old form of "ganymede."

CATASTROPHE, conclusion.

CATCHPOLE, sheriff's officer.

CATES, dainties, provisions.

CATSO, rogue, cheat.

CAUTELOUS, crafty, artful.

CENSURE, criticism; sentence.

CENSURE, criticise; pass sentence, doom.

CERUSE, cosmetic containing white lead.

CESS, assess.

CHANGE, "hunt --," follow a fresh scent.

CHAPMAN, retail dealer.

CHARACTER, handwriting.

CHARGE, expense.

CHARM, subdue with magic, lay a spell on, silence.

CHARMING, exercising magic power.

CHARTEL, challenge.

CHEAP, bargain, market.

CHEAR, CHEER, comfort, encouragement; food, entertainment.

CHECK AT, aim reproof at.

CHEQUIN, gold Italian coin.

CHEVRIL, from kidskin, which is elastic and pliable.

CHIAUS, Turkish envoy; used for a cheat, swindler.

CHILDERMASS DAY, Innocents' Day.

CHOKE-BAIL, action which does not allow of bail.

CHRYSOPOEIA, alchemy.

CHRYSOSPERM, ways of producing gold.

CIBATION, adding fresh substances to supply the waste of evaporation.

CIMICI, bugs.

CINOPER, cinnabar.

CIOPPINI, chopine, lady's high shoe.

CIRCLING BOY, "a species of roarer; one who in some way drew a man into a snare, to cheat or rob him" (Nares).

CIRCUMSTANCE, circumlocution, beating about the bush; ceremony, everything pertaining to a certain condition; detail, particular.

CITRONISE, turn citron colour.

CITTERN, kind of guitar.

CITY-WIRES, woman of fashion, who made use of wires for hair and dress.

CIVIL, legal.

CLAP, clack, chatter.

CLAPPER-DUDGEON, downright beggar.

CLAPS HIS DISH, a clap, or clack, dish (dish with a movable lid) was carried by beggars and lepers to show that the vessel was empty, and to give sound of their approach.

CLARIDIANA, heroine of an old romance.

CLARISSIMO, Venetian noble.

CLEM, starve.

CLICKET, latch.

CLIM O' THE CLOUGHS, etc., wordy heroes of romance.

CLIMATE, country.

CLOSE, secret, private; secretive.

CLOSENESS, secrecy.

CLOTH, arras, hangings.

CLOUT, mark shot at, bull's eye.

CLOWN, countryman, clodhopper.

COACH-LEAVES, folding blinds.

COALS, "bear no --," submit to no affront.

COAT-ARMOUR, coat of arms.

COAT-CARD, court-card.

COB-HERRING, HERRING-COB, a young herring.

COB-SWAN, male swan.

COCK-A-HOOP, denoting unstinted jollity; thought to be derived from turning on the tap that all might drink to the full of the flowing liquor.

COCKATRICE, reptile supposed to be produced from a cock's egg and to kill by its eye -- used as a term of reproach for a woman.

COCK-BRAINED, giddy, wild.

COCKER, pamper.

COCKSCOMB, fool's cap.

COCKSTONE, stone said to be found in a cock's gizzard, and to possess particular virtues.

CODLING, softening by boiling.

COFFIN, raised crust of a pie.

COG, cheat, wheedle.

COIL, turmoil, confusion, ado.

COKELY, master of a puppet-show (Whalley).

COKES, fool, gull.

COLD-CONCEITED, having cold opinion of, coldly affected towards.

COLE-HARBOUR, a retreat for people of all sorts.

COLLECTION, composure; deduction.

COLLOP, small slice, piece of flesh.

COLLY, blacken.

COLOUR, pretext.

COLOURS, "fear no --," no enemy (quibble).

COLSTAFF, cowlstaff, pole for carrying a cowl=tub.

COME ABOUT, charge, turn round.

COMFORTABLE BREAD, spiced gingerbread.

COMING, forward, ready to respond, complaisant.

COMMENT, commentary; "sometime it is taken for a lie or fayned tale" (Bullokar, 1616).

COMMODITY, "current for --," allusion to practice of money-lenders, who forced the borrower to take part of the loan in the shape of worthless goods on which the latter had to make money if he could.

COMMUNICATE, share.

COMPASS, "in --," within the range, sphere.

COMPLEMENT, completion, completement; anything required for the perfecting or carrying out of a person or affair; accomplishment.

COMPLEXION, natural disposition, constitution.

COMPLIMENT, See Complement.

COMPLIMENTARIES, masters of accomplishments.

COMPOSITION, constitution; agreement, contract.

COMPOSURE, composition.

COMPTER, COUNTER, debtors' prison.

CONCEALMENT, a certain amount of church property had been retained at the dissolution of the monasteries; Elizabeth sent commissioners to search it out, and the courtiers begged for it.

CONCEIT, idea, fancy, witty invention, conception, opinion.

CONCEIT, apprehend.

CONCEITED, fancifully, ingeniously devised or conceived; possessed of intelligence, witty, ingenious (hence well conceited, etc.); disposed to joke; of opinion, possessed of an idea.

CONCEIVE, understand.

CONCENT, harmony, agreement.

CONCLUDE, infer, prove.

CONCOCT, assimilate, digest.

CONDEN'T, probably conducted.

CONDUCT, escort, conductor.

CONEY-CATCH, cheat.

CONFECT, sweetmeat.

CONFER, compare.

CONGIES, bows.

CONNIVE, give a look, wink, of secret intelligence.

CONSORT, company, concert.

CONSTANCY, fidelity, ardour, persistence.

CONSTANT, confirmed, persistent, faithful.

CONSTANTLY, firmly, persistently.

CONTEND, strive.

CONTINENT, holding together.

CONTROL (the point), bear or beat down.

CONVENT, assembly, meeting.

CONVERT, turn (oneself).

CONVEY, transmit from one to another.

CONVINCE, evince, prove; overcome, overpower; convict.

COP, head, top; tuft on head of birds; "a cop" may have reference to one or other meaning; Gifford and others interpret as "conical, terminating in a point."

COPE-MAN, chapman.

COPESMATE, companion.

COPY (Lat. copia), abundance, copiousness.

CORN ("powder --"), grain.

COROLLARY, finishing part or touch.

CORSIVE, corrosive.

CORTINE, curtain, (arch.) wall between two towers, etc.

CORYAT, famous for his travels, published as "Coryat's Crudities."

COSSET, pet lamb, pet.

COSTARD, head.

COSTARD-MONGER, apple-seller, coster-monger.

COSTS, ribs.

COTE, hut.

COTHURNAL, from "cothurnus," a particular boot worn by actors in Greek tragedy.

COTQUEAN, hussy.

COUNSEL, secret.

COUNTENANCE, means necessary for support; credit, standing.

COUNTER. See Compter.

COUNTER, pieces of metal or ivory for calculating at play.

COUNTER, "hunt --," follow scent in reverse direction.

COUNTERFEIT, false coin.

COUNTERPANE, one part or counterpart of a deed or indenture.

COUNTERPOINT, opposite, contrary point.

COURT-DISH, a kind of drinking-cup (Halliwell); N.E.D. quotes from Bp. Goodman's "Court of James I.": "The king...caused his carver to cut him out a court-dish, that is, something of every dish, which he sent him as part of his reversion," but this does not sound like short allowance or small receptacle.

COURT-DOR, fool.

COURTEAU, curtal, small horse with docked tail.

COURTSHIP, courtliness.

COVETISE, avarice.

COWSHARD, cow dung.

COXCOMB, fool's cap, fool.

COY, shrink; disdain.

COYSTREL, low varlet.

COZEN, cheat.

CRACK, lively young rogue, wag.

CRACK, crack up, boast; come to grief.

CRAMBE, game of crambo, in which the players find rhymes for a given word.

CRANCH, craunch.

CRANION, spider-like; also fairy appellation for a fly (Gifford, who refers to lines in Drayton's "Nimphidia").

CRIMP, game at cards.

CRINCLE, draw back, turn aside.

CRISPED, with curled or waved hair.

CROP, gather, reap.

CROPSHIRE, a kind of herring. (See N.E.D.)

CROSS, any piece of money, many coins being stamped with a cross.

CROSS AND PILE, heads and tails.

CROSSLET, crucible.

CROWD, fiddle.

CRUDITIES, undigested matter.

CRUMP, curl up.

CRUSADO, Portuguese gold coin, marked with a cross.

CRY ("he that cried Italian"), "speak in a musical cadence," intone, or declaim (?); cry up.

CUCKING-STOOL, used for the ducking of scolds, etc.

CUCURBITE, a gourd-shaped vessel used for distillation.

CUERPO, "in --," in undress.

CULLICE, broth.

CULLION, base fellow, coward.

CULLISEN, badge worn on their arm by servants.

CULVERIN, kind of cannon.

CUNNING, skill.

CUNNING, skilful.

CUNNING-MAN, fortune-teller.

CURE, care for.

CURIOUS(LY), scrupulous, particular; elaborate, elegant(ly), dainty(ly) (hence "in curious").

CURST, shrewish, mischievous.

CURTAL, dog with docked tail, of inferior sort.

CUSTARD, "quaking --," " -- politic," reference to a large custard which formed part of a city feast and afforded huge entertainment, for the fool jumped into it, and other like tricks were played. (See "All's Well, etc." ii. 5, 40.)

CUTWORK, embroidery, open-work.

CYPRES (CYPRUS) (quibble), cypress (or cyprus) being a transparent material, and when black used for mourning.

DAGGER (" -- frumety"), name of tavern.

DARGISON, apparently some person known in ballad or tale.

DAUPHIN MY BOY, refrain of old comic song.

DAW, daunt.

DEAD LIFT, desperate emergency.

DEAR, applied to that which in any way touches us nearly.

DECLINE, turn off from; turn away, aside.

DEFALK, deduct, abate.

DEFEND, forbid.

DEGENEROUS, degenerate.

DEGREES, steps.

DELATE, accuse.

DEMI-CULVERIN, cannon carrying a ball of about ten pounds.

DENIER, the smallest possible coin, being the twelfth part of a sou.

DEPART, part with.

DEPENDANCE, ground of quarrel in duello language.

DESERT, reward.

DESIGNMENT, design.

DESPERATE, rash, reckless.

DETECT, allow to be detected, betray, inform against.

DETERMINE, terminate.

DETRACT, draw back, refuse.

DEVICE, masque, show; a thing moved by wires, etc., puppet.

DEVISE, exact in every particular.

DEVISED, invented.

DIAPASM, powdered aromatic herbs, made into balls of perfumed paste. (See Pomander.)

DIBBLE, (?) moustache (N.E.D.); (?) dagger (Cunningham).

DIFFUSED, disordered, scattered, irregular.

DIGHT, dressed.

DILDO, refrain of popular songs; vague term of low meaning.

DIMBLE, dingle, ravine.

DIMENSUM, stated allowance.

DISBASE, debase.

DISCERN, distinguish, show a difference between.

DISCHARGE, settle for.

DISCIPLINE, reformation; ecclesiastical system.

DISCLAIM, renounce all part in.

DISCOURSE, process of reasoning, reasoning faculty.

DISCOURTSHIP, discourtesy.

DISCOVER, betray, reveal; display.

DISFAVOUR, disfigure.

DISPARAGEMENT, legal term applied to the unfitness in any way of a marriage arranged for in the case of wards.

DISPENSE WITH, grant dispensation for.

DISPLAY, extend.

DIS'PLE, discipline, teach by the whip.

DISPOSED, inclined to merriment.

DISPOSURE, disposal.

DISPRISE, depreciate.

DISPUNCT, not punctilious.

DISQUISITION, search.

DISSOLVED, enervated by grief.

DISTANCE, (?) proper measure.

DISTASTE, offence, cause of offence.

DISTASTE, render distasteful.

DISTEMPERED, upset, out of humour.

DIVISION (mus.), variation, modulation.

DOG-BOLT, term of contempt.

DOLE, given in dole, charity.

DOLE OF FACES, distribution of grimaces.

DOOM, verdict, sentence.

DOP, dip, low bow.

DOR, beetle, buzzing insect, drone, idler.

DOR, (?) buzz; "give the --," make a fool of.

DOSSER, pannier, basket.

DOTES, endowments, qualities.

DOTTEREL, plover; gull, fool.

DOUBLE, behave deceitfully.

DOXY, wench, mistress.

DRACHM, Greek silver coin.

DRESS, groom, curry.

DRESSING, coiffure.

DRIFT, intention.

DRYFOOT, track by mere scent of foot.

DUCKING, punishment for minor offences.

DUILL, grieve.

DUMPS, melancholy, originally a mournful melody.

DURINDANA, Orlando's sword.

DWINDLE, shrink away, be overawed.

EAN, yean, bring forth young.

EASINESS, readiness.

EBOLITION, ebullition.

EDGE, sword.

EECH, eke.

EGREGIOUS, eminently excellent.

EKE, also, moreover.

E-LA, highest note in the scale.

EGGS ON THE SPIT, important business on hand.

ELF-LOCK, tangled hair, supposed to be the work of elves.

EMMET, ant.

ENGAGE, involve.

ENGHLE. See Ingle.

ENGHLE, cajole; fondle.

ENGIN(E), device, contrivance; agent; ingenuity, wit.

ENGINER, engineer, deviser, plotter.

ENGINOUS, crafty, full of devices; witty, ingenious.

ENGROSS, monopolise.

ENS, an existing thing, a substance.

ENSIGNS, tokens, wounds.

ENSURE, assure.

ENTERTAIN, take into service.

ENTREAT, plead.

ENTREATY, entertainment.

ENTRY, place where a deer has lately passed.

ENVOY, denouement, conclusion.

ENVY, spite, calumny, dislike, odium.

EPHEMERIDES, calendars.

EQUAL, just, impartial.

ERECTION, elevation in esteem.

ERINGO, candied root of the sea-holly, formerly used as a sweetmeat and aphrodisiac.

ERRANT, arrant.

ESSENTIATE, become assimilated.

ESTIMATION, esteem.

ESTRICH, ostrich.

ETHNIC, heathen.

EURIPUS, flux and reflux.

EVEN, just equable.

EVENT, fate, issue.

EVENT(ED), issue(d).

EVERT, overturn.

EXACUATE, sharpen.

EXAMPLESS, without example or parallel.

EXCALIBUR, King Arthur's sword.

EXEMPLIFY, make an example of.

EXEMPT, separate, exclude.

EXEQUIES, obsequies.

EXHALE, drag out.

EXHIBITION, allowance for keep, pocket-money.

EXORBITANT, exceeding limits of propriety or law, inordinate.

EXORNATION, ornament.

EXPECT, wait.

EXPIATE, terminate.

EXPLICATE, explain, unfold.

EXTEMPORAL, extempore, unpremeditated.

EXTRACTION, essence.

EXTRAORDINARY, employed for a special or temporary purpose.

EXTRUDE, expel.

EYE, "in --," in view.

EYEBRIGHT, (?) a malt liquor in which the herb of this name was infused, or a person who sold the same (Gifford).

EYE-TINGE, least shade or gleam.

FACE, appearance.

FACES ABOUT, military word of command.

FACINOROUS, extremely wicked.

FACKINGS, faith.

FACT, deed, act, crime.

FACTIOUS, seditious, belonging to a party, given to party feeling.

FAECES, dregs.

FAGIOLI, French beans.

FAIN, forced, necessitated.

FAITHFUL, believing.

FALL, ruff or band turned back on the shoulders; or, veil.

FALSIFY, feign (fencing term).

FAME, report.

FAMILIAR, attendant spirit.

FANTASTICAL, capricious, whimsical.

FARCE, stuff.

FAR-FET. See Fet.

FARTHINGAL, hooped petticoat.

FAUCET, tapster.

FAULT, lack; loss, break in line of scent; "for --," in default of.

FAUTOR, partisan.

FAYLES, old table game similar to backgammon.

FEAR(ED), affright(ed).

FEAT, activity, operation; deed, action.

FEAT, elegant, trim.

FEE, "in --" by feudal obligation.

FEIZE, beat, belabour.

FELLOW, term of contempt.

FENNEL, emblem of flattery.

FERE, companion, fellow.

FERN-SEED, supposed to have power of rendering invisible.

FET, fetched.

FETCH, trick.

FEUTERER (Fr. vautrier), dog-keeper.

FEWMETS, dung.

FICO, fig.

FIGGUM, (?) jugglery.

FIGMENT, fiction, invention.

FIRK, frisk, move suddenly, or in jerks; "-- up," stir up, rouse; "firks mad," suddenly behaves like a madman.

FIT, pay one out, punish.

FITNESS, readiness.

FITTON (FITTEN), lie, invention.

FIVE-AND-FIFTY, "highest number to stand on at

primero" (Gifford).

FLAG, to fly low and waveringly.

FLAGON CHAIN, for hanging a smelling-bottle (Fr. flacon) round the neck (?). (See N.E.D.).

FLAP-DRAGON, game similar to snap-dragon.

FLASKET, some kind of basket.

FLAW, sudden gust or squall of wind.

FLAWN, custard.

FLEA, catch fleas.

FLEER, sneer, laugh derisively.

FLESH, feed a hawk or dog with flesh to incite it to the chase; initiate in blood-shed; satiate.

FLICKER-MOUSE, bat.

FLIGHT, light arrow.

FLITTER-MOUSE, bat.

FLOUT, mock, speak and act contemptuously.

FLOWERS, pulverised substance.

FLY, familiar spirit.

FOIL, weapon used in fencing; that which sets anything off to advantage.

FOIST, cut-purse, sharper.

FOND(LY), foolish(ly).

FOOT-CLOTH, housings of ornamental cloth which hung down on either side a horse to the ground.

FOOTING, foothold; footstep; dancing.

FOPPERY, foolery.

FOR, "-- failing," for fear of failing.

FORBEAR, bear with; abstain from.

FORCE, "hunt at --," run the game down with dogs.

FOREHEAD, modesty; face, assurance, effrontery.

FORESLOW, delay.

FORESPEAK, bewitch; foretell.

FORETOP, front lock of hair which fashion required to be worn upright.

FORGED, fabricated.

FORM, state formally.

FORMAL, shapely; normal; conventional.

FORTHCOMING, produced when required.

FOUNDER, disable with over-riding.

FOURM, form, lair.

FOX, sword.

FRAIL, rush basket in which figs or raisins were packed.

FRAMPULL, peevish, sour-tempered.

FRAPLER, blusterer, wrangler.

FRAYING, "a stag is said to fray his head when he rubs it against a tree to...cause the outward coat of the new horns to fall off" (Gifford).

FREIGHT (of the gazetti), burden (of the newspapers).

FREQUENT, full.

FRICACE, rubbing.

FRICATRICE, woman of low character.

FRIPPERY, old clothes shop.

FROCK, smock-frock.

FROLICS, (?) humorous verses circulated at a feast (N.E.D.); couplets wrapped round sweetmeats (Cunningham).

FRONTLESS, shameless.

FROTED, rubbed.

FRUMETY, hulled wheat boiled in milk and spiced.

FRUMP, flout, sneer.

FUCUS, dye.

FUGEAND, (?) figent: fidgety, restless (N.E.D.).

FULLAM, false dice.

FULMART, polecat.

FULSOME, foul, offensive.

FURIBUND, raging, furious.

GALLEY-FOIST, city-barge, used on Lord Mayor's Day, when he was sworn into his office at Westminster (Whalley).

GALLIARD, lively dance in triple time.

GAPE, be eager after.

GARAGANTUA, Rabelais' giant.

GARB, sheaf (Fr. gerbe); manner, fashion, behaviour.

GARD, guard, trimming, gold or silver lace, or other ornament.

GARDED, faced or trimmed.

GARNISH, fee.

GAVEL-KIND, name of a land-tenure existing chiefly in Kent; from 16th century often used to denote custom of dividing a deceased man's property equally among his sons (N.E.D.).

GAZETTE, small Venetian coin worth about three-farthings.

GEANCE, jaunt, errand.

GEAR (GEER), stuff, matter, affair.

GELID, frozen.

GEMONIES, steps from which the bodies of criminals were thrown into the river.

GENERAL, free, affable.

GENIUS, attendant spirit.

GENTRY, gentlemen; manners characteristic of gentry, good breeding.

GIB-CAT, tom-cat.

GIGANTOMACHIZE, start a giants' war.

GIGLOT, wanton.

GIMBLET, gimlet.

GING, gang.

GLASS ("taking in of shadows, etc."), crystal or beryl.

GLEEK, card game played by three; party of three, trio; side glance.

GLICK (GLEEK), jest, gibe.

GLIDDER, glaze.

GLORIOUSLY, of vain glory.

GODWIT, bird of the snipe family.

GOLD-END-MAN, a buyer of broken gold and silver.

GOLL, hand.

GONFALIONIER, standard-bearer, chief magistrate, etc.

GOOD, sound in credit.

GOOD-YEAR, good luck.

GOOSE-TURD, colour of. (See Turd).

GORCROW, carrion crow.

GORGET, neck armour.

GOSSIP, godfather.

GOWKED, from "gowk," to stand staring and gaping like a fool.

GRANNAM, grandam.

GRASS, (?) grease, fat.

GRATEFUL, agreeable, welcome.

GRATIFY, give thanks to.

GRATITUDE, gratuity.

GRATULATE, welcome, congratulate.

GRAVITY, dignity.

GRAY, badger.

GRICE, cub.

GRIEF, grievance.

GRIPE, vulture, griffin.

GRIPE'S EGG, vessel in shape of.

GROAT, fourpence.

GROGRAN, coarse stuff made of silk and mohair, or of coarse silk.

GROOM-PORTER, officer in the royal household.

GROPE, handle, probe.

GROUND, pit (hence "grounded judgments").

GUARD, caution, heed.

GUARDANT, heraldic term: turning the head only.

GUILDER, Dutch coin worth about 4d.

GULES, gullet, throat; heraldic term for red.

GULL, simpleton, dupe.

GUST, taste.

HAB NAB, by, on, chance.

HABERGEON, coat of mail.

HAGGARD, wild female hawk; hence coy, wild.

HALBERD, combination of lance and battle-axe.

HALL, "a --!" a cry to clear the room for the dancers.

HANDSEL, first money taken.

HANGER, loop or strap on a sword-belt from which the sword was suspended.

HAP, fortune, luck.

HAPPILY, haply.

HAPPINESS, appropriateness, fitness.

HAPPY, rich.

HARBOUR, track, trace (an animal) to its shelter.

HARD-FAVOURED, harsh-featured.

HARPOCRATES, Horus the child, son of Osiris, figured with a finger pointing to his mouth, indicative of silence.

HARRINGTON, a patent was granted to Lord H. for the coinage of tokens (q.v.).

HARROT, herald.

HARRY NICHOLAS, founder of a community called the "Family of Love".

HAY, net for catching rabbits, etc.

HAY! (Ital. hai!), you have it (a fencing term).

HAY IN HIS HORN, ill-tempered person.

HAZARD, game at dice; that which is staked.

HEAD, "first --," young deer with antlers first sprouting; fig. a newly-ennobled man.

HEADBOROUGH, constable.

HEARKEN AFTER, inquire; "hearken out," find, search out.

HEARTEN, encourage.

HEAVEN AND HELL ("Alchemist"), names of taverns.

HECTIC, fever.

HEDGE IN, include.

HELM, upper part of a retort.

HER'NSEW, hernshaw, heron.

HIERONIMO (JERONIMO), hero of Kyd's "Spanish Tragedy."

HOBBY, nag.

HOBBY-HORSE, imitation horse of some light material, fastened round the waist of the morrice-dancer, who imitated the movements of a skittish horse.

HODDY-DODDY, fool.

HOIDEN, hoyden, formerly applied to both sexes (ancient term for leveret? Gifford).

HOLLAND, name of two famous chemists.

HONE AND HONERO, wailing expressions of lament or discontent.

HOOD-WINK'D, blindfolded.

HORARY, hourly.

HORN-MAD, stark mad (quibble).

HORN-THUMB, cut-purses were in the habit of wearing a horn shield on the thumb.

HORSE-BREAD-EATING, horses were often fed on coarse bread.

HORSE-COURSER, horse-dealer.

HOSPITAL, Christ's Hospital.

HOWLEGLAS, Eulenspiegel, the hero of a popular German tale which relates his buffooneries and knavish tricks.

HUFF, hectoring, arrogance.

HUFF IT, swagger.

HUISHER (Fr. huissier), usher.

HUM, beer and spirits mixed together.

HUMANITIAN, humanist, scholar.

HUMOROUS, capricious, moody, out of humour; moist.

HUMOUR, a word used in and out of season in the time of Shakespeare and Ben Jonson, and ridiculed by both.

HUMOURS, manners.

HUMPHREY, DUKE, those who were dinnerless spent the dinner-hour in a part of St. Paul's where stood a monument said to be that of the duke's; hence "dine with Duke Humphrey," to go hungry.

HURTLESS, harmless.

IDLE, useless, unprofitable.

ILL-AFFECTED, ill-disposed.

ILL-HABITED, unhealthy.

ILLUSTRATE, illuminate.

IMBIBITION, saturation, steeping.

IMBROCATA, fencing term: a thrust in tierce.

IMPAIR, impairment.

IMPART, give money.

IMPARTER, any one ready to be cheated and to part with his money.

IMPEACH, damage.

IMPERTINENCIES, irrelevancies.

IMPERTINENT(LY), irrelevant(ly), without reason or purpose.

IMPOSITION, duty imposed by.

IMPOTENTLY, beyond power of control.

IMPRESS, money in advance.

IMPULSION, incitement.

IN AND IN, a game played by two or three persons with four dice.

INCENSE, incite, stir up.

INCERATION, act of covering with wax; or reducing a substance to softness of wax.

INCH, "to their --es," according to their stature, capabilities.

INCH-PIN, sweet-bread.

INCONVENIENCE, inconsistency, absurdity.

INCONY, delicate, rare (used as a term of affection).

INCUBEE, incubus.

INCUBUS, evil spirit that oppresses us in sleep, nightmare.

INCURIOUS, unfastidious, uncritical.

INDENT, enter into engagement.

INDIFFERENT, tolerable, passable.

INDIGESTED, shapeless, chaotic.

INDUCE, introduce.

INDUE, supply.

INEXORABLE, relentless.

INFANTED, born, produced.

INFLAME, augment charge.

INGENIOUS, used indiscriminantly for ingenuous; intelligent, talented.

INGENUITY, ingenuousness.

INGENUOUS, generous.

INGINE. See Engin.

INGINER, engineer. (See Enginer).

INGLE, OR ENGHLE, bosom friend, intimate, minion.

INHABITABLE, uninhabitable.

INJURY, insult, affront.

IN-MATE, resident, indwelling.

INNATE, natural.

INNOCENT, simpleton.

INQUEST, jury, or other official body of inquiry.

INQUISITION, inquiry.

INSTANT, immediate.

INSTRUMENT, legal document.

INSURE, assure.

INTEGRATE, complete, perfect.

INTELLIGENCE, secret information, news.

INTEND, note carefully, attend, give ear to, be occupied with.

INTENDMENT, intention.

INTENT, intention, wish.

INTENTION, concentration of attention or gaze.

INTENTIVE, attentive.

INTERESSED, implicated.

INTRUDE, bring in forcibly or without leave.

INVINCIBLY, invisibly.

INWARD, intimate.

IRPE (uncertain), "a fantastic grimace, or contortion of the body: (Gifford).

JACK, Jack o' the clock, automaton figure that strikes the hour; Jack-a-lent, puppet thrown at in Lent.

JACK, key of a virginal.

JACOB'S STAFF, an instrument for taking altitudes and distances.

JADE, befool.

JEALOUSY, JEALOUS, suspicion, suspicious.

JERKING, lashing.

JEW'S TRUMP, Jew's harp.

JIG, merry ballad or tune; a fanciful dialogue or light comic act introduced at the end or during an interlude of a play.

JOINED (JOINT)-STOOL, folding stool.

JOLL, jowl.

JOLTHEAD, blockhead.

JUMP, agree, tally.

JUST YEAR, no one was capable of the consulship until he was forty-three.

KELL, cocoon.

KELLY, an alchemist.

KEMB, comb.

KEMIA, vessel for distillation.

KIBE, chap, sore.

KILDERKIN, small barrel.

KILL, kiln.

KIND, nature; species; "do one's --," act according to one's nature.

KIRTLE, woman's gown of jacket and petticoat.

KISS OR DRINK AFORE ME, "this is a familiar expression, employed when what the speaker is just about to say is anticipated by another" (Gifford).

KIT, fiddle.

KNACK, snap, click.

KNIPPER-DOLING, a well-known Anabaptist.

KNITTING CUP, marriage cup.

KNOCKING, striking, weighty.

KNOT, company, band; a sandpiper or robin snipe (Tringa canutus); flower-bed laid out in fanciful design.

KURSINED, KYRSIN, christened.

LABOURED, wrought with labour and care.

LADE, load(ed).

LADING, load.

LAID, plotted.

LANCE-KNIGHT (Lanzknecht), a German mercenary foot-soldier.

LAP, fold.

LAR, household god.

LARD, garnish.

LARGE, abundant.

LARUM, alarum, call to arms.

LATTICE, tavern windows were furnished with lattices of various colours.

LAUNDER, to wash gold in aqua regia, so as imperceptibly to extract some of it.

LAVE, ladle, bale.

LAW, "give --," give a start (term of chase).

LAXATIVE, loose.

LAY ABOARD, run alongside generally with intent to board.

LEAGUER, siege, or camp of besieging army.

LEASING, lying.

LEAVE, leave off, desist.

LEER, leering or "empty, hence, perhaps, leer horse, a horse without a rider; leer is an adjective meaning uncontrolled, hence 'leer drunkards'" (Halliwell); according to Nares, a leer (empty) horse meant also a led horse; leeward, left.

LEESE, lose.

LEGS, "make --," do obeisance.

LEIGER, resident representative.

LEIGERITY, legerdemain.

LEMMA, subject proposed, or title of the epigram.

LENTER, slower.

LET, hinder.

LET, hindrance.

LEVEL COIL, a rough game...in which one hunted another from his seat. Hence used for any noisy riot (Halliwell).

LEWD, ignorant.

LEYSTALLS, receptacles of filth.

LIBERAL, ample.

LIEGER, ledger, register.

LIFT(ING), steal(ing); theft.

LIGHT, alight.

LIGHTLY, commonly, usually, often.

LIKE, please.

LIKELY, agreeable, pleasing.

LIME-HOUND, leash-, blood-hound.

LIMMER, vile, worthless.

LIN, leave off.

Line, "by --," by rule.

LINSTOCK, staff to stick in the ground, with forked head to hold a lighted match for firing cannon.

LIQUID, clear.

LIST, listen, hark; like, please.

LIVERY, legal term, delivery of the possession, etc.

LOGGET, small log, stick.

LOOSE, solution; upshot, issue; release of an arrow.

LOSE, give over, desist from; waste.

LOUTING, bowing, cringing.

LUCULENT, bright of beauty.

LUDGATHIANS, dealers on Ludgate Hill.

LURCH, rob, cheat.

LUTE, to close a vessel with some kind of cement.

MACK, unmeaning expletive.

MADGE-HOWLET or OWL, barn-owl.

MAIM, hurt, injury.

MAIN, chief concern (used as a quibble on heraldic term for "hand").

MAINPRISE, becoming surety for a prisoner so as to procure his release.

MAINTENANCE, giving aid, or abetting.

MAKE, mate.

MAKE, MADE, acquaint with business, prepare(d), instruct(ed).

MALLANDERS, disease of horses.

MALT HORSE, dray horse.

MAMMET, puppet.

MAMMOTHREPT, spoiled child.

MANAGE, control (term used for breaking-in horses); handling, administration.

MANGO, slave-dealer.

MANGONISE, polish up for sale.

MANIPLES, bundles, handfuls.

MANKIND, masculine, like a virago.

MANKIND, humanity.

MAPLE FACE, spotted face (N.E.D.).

MARCHPANE, a confection of almonds, sugar, etc.

MARK, "fly to the --," "generally said of a goshawk when, having 'put in' a covey of partridges, she takes stand, marking the spot where they disappeared from view until the falconer arrives to put them out to her" (Harting, Bibl. Accip. Gloss. 226).

MARLE, marvel.

MARROW-BONE MAN, one often on his knees for prayer.

MARRY! exclamation derived from the Virgin's name.

MARRY GIP, "probably originated from By Mary Gipcy = St. Mary of Egypt, (N.E.D.).

MARTAGAN, Turk's cap lily.

MARYHINCHCO, stringhalt.

MASORETH, Masora, correct form of the scriptural text according to Hebrew tradition.

MASS, abb. for master.

MAUND, beg.

MAUTHER, girl, maid.

MEAN, moderation.

MEASURE, dance, more especially a stately one.

MEAT, "carry -- in one's mouth," be a source of money or entertainment.

MEATH, metheglin.

MECHANICAL, belonging to mechanics, mean, vulgar.

MEDITERRANEO, middle aisle of St. Paul's, a general resort for business and amusement.

MEET WITH, even with.

MELICOTTON, a late kind of peach.

MENSTRUE, solvent.

MERCAT, market.

MERD, excrement.

MERE, undiluted; absolute, unmitigated.

MESS, party of four.

METHEGLIN, fermented liquor, of which one ingredient was honey.

METOPOSCOPY, study of physiognomy.

MIDDLING GOSSIP, go-between.

MIGNIARD, dainty, delicate.

MILE-END, training-ground of the city.

MINE-MEN, sappers.

MINION, form of cannon.

MINSITIVE, (?) mincing, affected (N.E.D.).

MISCELLANY MADAM, "a female trader in miscellaneous articles; a dealer in trinkets or ornaments of various kinds, such as kept shops in the New Exchange" (Nares).

MISCELLINE, mixed grain; medley.

MISCONCEIT, misconception.

MISPRISE, MISPRISION, mistake, misunderstanding.

MISTAKE AWAY, carry away as if by mistake.

MITHRIDATE, an antidote against poison.

MOCCINIGO, small Venetian coin, worth about ninepence.

MODERN, in the mode; ordinary, commonplace.

MOMENT, force or influence of value.

MONTANTO, upward stroke.

MONTH'S MIND, violent desire.

MOORISH, like a moor or waste.

MORGLAY, sword of Bevis of Southampton.

MORRICE-DANCE, dance on May Day, etc., in which certain personages were represented.

MORTALITY, death.

MORT-MAL, old sore, gangrene.

MOSCADINO, confection flavoured with musk.

MOTHER, Hysterica passio.

MOTION, proposal, request; puppet, puppet-show; "one of the small figures on the face of a large clock which was moved by the vibration of the pendulum" (Whalley).

MOTION, suggest, propose.

MOTLEY, parti-coloured dress of a fool; hence used to signify pertaining to, or like, a fool.

MOTTE, motto.

MOURNIVAL, set of four aces or court cards in a hand; a quartette.

MOW, setord hay or sheaves of grain.

MUCH! expressive of irony and incredulity.

MUCKINDER, handkerchief.

MULE, "born to ride on --," judges or serjeants-at-law formerly rode on mules when going in state to Westminster (Whally).

MULLETS, small pincers.

MUM-CHANCE, game of chance, played in silence.

MUN, must.

MUREY, dark crimson red.

MUSCOVY-GLASS, mica.

MUSE, wonder.

MUSICAL, in harmony.

MUSS, mouse; scramble.

MYROBOLANE, foreign conserve, "a dried plum, brought from the Indies".

MYSTERY, art, trade, profession.

NAIL, "to the --" (ad unguem), to perfection, to the very utmost.

NATIVE, natural.

NEAT, cattle.

NEAT, smartly apparelled; unmixed; dainty.

NEATLY, neatly finished.

NEATNESS, elegance.

NEIS, nose, scent.

NEUF (NEAF, NEIF), fist.

NEUFT, newt.

NIAISE, foolish, inexperienced person.

NICE, fastidious, trivial, finical, scrupulous.

NICENESS, fastidiousness.

NICK, exact amount; right moment; "set in the --," meaning uncertain.

NICE, suit, fit; hit, seize the right moment, etc., exactly hit on, hit off.

NOBLE, gold coin worth 6s. 8d.

NOCENT, harmful.

NIL, not will.

NOISE, company of musicians.

NOMENTACK, an Indian chief from Virginia.

NONES, nonce.

NOTABLE, egregious.

NOTE, sign, token.

NOUGHT, "be --," go to the devil, be hanged, etc.

NOWT-HEAD, blockhead.

NUMBER, rhythm.

NUPSON, oaf, simpleton.

OADE, woad.

OBARNI, preparation of mead.

OBJECT, oppose; expose; interpose.

OBLATRANT, barking, railing.

OBNOXIOUS, liable, exposed; offensive.

OBSERVANCE, homage, devoted service.

OBSERVANT, attentive, obsequious.

OBSERVE, show deference, respect.

OBSERVER, one who shows deference, or waits upon another.

OBSTANCY, legal phrase, "juridical opposition."

OBSTREPEROUS, clamorous, vociferous.

OBSTUPEFACT, stupefied.

ODLING, (?) "must have some relation to tricking and cheating" (Nares).

OMINOUS, deadly, fatal.

ONCE, at once; for good and all; used also for additional emphasis.

ONLY, pre-eminent, special.

OPEN, make public; expound.

OPPILATION, obstruction.

OPPONE, oppose.

OPPOSITE, antagonist.

OPPRESS, suppress.

ORIGINOUS, native.

ORT, remnant, scrap.

OUT, "to be --," to have forgotten one's part; not at one with each other.

OUTCRY, sale by auction.

OUTRECUIDANCE, arrogance, presumption.

OUTSPEAK, speak more than.

OVERPARTED, given too difficult a part to play.

OWLSPIEGEL. See Howleglass.

OYEZ! (O YES!), hear ye! call of the public crier when about to make a proclamation.

PACKING PENNY, "give a --," dismiss, send packing.

PAD, highway.

PAD-HORSE, road-horse.

PAINED (PANED) SLOPS, full breeches made of strips of different colour and material.

PAINFUL, diligent, painstaking.

PAINT, blush.

PALINODE, ode of recantation.

PALL, weaken, dim, make stale.

PALM, triumph.

PAN, skirt of dress or coat.

PANNEL, pad, or rough kind of saddle.

PANNIER-ALLY, inhabited by tripe-sellers.

PANNIER-MAN, hawker; a man employed about the inns of court to bring in provisions, set the table, etc.

PANTOFLE, indoor shoe, slipper.

PARAMENTOS, fine trappings.

PARANOMASIE, a play upon words.

PARANTORY, (?) peremptory.

PARCEL, particle, fragment (used contemptuously); article.

PARCEL, part, partly.

PARCEL-POET, poetaster.

PARERGA, subordinate matters.

PARGET, to paint or plaster the face.

PARLE, parley.

PARLOUS, clever, shrewd.

PART, apportion.

PARTAKE, participate in.

PARTED, endowed, talented.

PARTICULAR, individual person.

PARTIZAN, kind of halberd.

PARTRICH, partridge.

PARTS, qualities, endowments.

PASH, dash, smash.

PASS, care, trouble oneself.

PASSADO, fencing term: a thrust.

PASSAGE, game at dice.

PASSINGLY, exceedingly.

PASSION, effect caused by external agency.

PASSION, "in --," in so melancholy a tone, so pathetically.

PATOUN, (?) Fr. Paton, pellet of dough; perhaps the "moulding of the tobacco...for the pipe" (Gifford); (?) variant of Petun, South American name of tobacco.

PATRICO, the recorder, priest, orator of strolling beggars or gipsies.

PATTEN, shoe with wooden sole; "go --," keep step with, accompany.

PAUCA VERBA, few words.

PAVIN, a stately dance.

PEACE, "with my master's --," by leave, favour.

PECULIAR, individual, single.

PEDANT, teacher of the languages.

PEEL, baker's shovel.

PEEP, speak in a small or shrill voice.

PEEVISH(LY), foolish(ly), capricious(ly); childish(ly).

PELICAN, a retort fitted with tube or tubes, for continuous distillation.

PENCIL, small tuft of hair.

PERDUE, soldier accustomed to hazardous service.

PEREMPTORY, resolute, bold; imperious; thorough, utter, absolute(ly).

PERIMETER, circumference of a figure.

PERIOD, limit, end.

PERK, perk up.

PERPETUANA, "this seems to be that glossy kind of stuff now called everlasting, and anciently worn by serjeants and other city officers" (Gifford).

PERSPECTIVE, a view, scene or scenery; an optical device which gave a distortion to the picture unless seen from a particular point; a relief, modelled to produce an optical illusion.

PERSPICIL, optic glass.

PERSTRINGE, criticise, censure.

PERSUADE, inculcate, commend.

PERSWAY, mitigate.

PERTINACY, pertinacity.

PESTLING, pounding, pulverising, like a pestle.

PETASUS, broad-brimmed hat or winged cap worn by Mercury.

PETITIONARY, supplicatory.

PETRONEL, a kind of carbine or light gun carried by horsemen.

PETULANT, pert, insolent.

PHERE. See Fere.

PHLEGMA, watery distilled liquor (old chem. "water").

PHRENETIC, madman.

PICARDIL, stiff upright collar fastened on to the coat (Whalley).

PICT-HATCH, disreputable quarter of London.

PIECE, person, used for woman or girl; a gold coin worth in Jonson's time 20s. or 22s.

PIECES OF EIGHT, Spanish coin: piastre equal to eight reals.

PIED, variegated.

PIE-POUDRES (Fr. pied-poudreux, dusty-foot), court held at fairs to administer justice to itinerant vendors and buyers.

PILCHER, term of contempt; one who wore a buff or leather jerkin, as did the serjeants of the counter; a pilferer.

PILED, pilled, peeled, bald.

PILL'D, polled, fleeced.

PIMLICO, "sometimes spoken of as a person -- perhaps master of a house famous for a particular ale" (Gifford).

PINE, afflict, distress.

PINK, stab with a weapon; pierce or cut in scallops for ornament.

PINNACE, a go-between in infamous sense.

PISMIRE, ant.

PISTOLET, gold coin, worth about 6s.

PITCH, height of a bird of prey's flight.

PLAGUE, punishment, torment.

PLAIN, lament.

PLAIN SONG, simple melody.

PLAISE, plaice.

PLANET, "struck with a --," planets were supposed to have powers of blasting or exercising secret influences.

PLAUSIBLE, pleasing.

PLAUSIBLY, approvingly.

PLOT, plan.

PLY, apply oneself to.

POESIE, posy, motto inside a ring.

POINT IN HIS DEVICE, exact in every particular.

POINTS, tagged laces or cords for fastening the breeches to the doublet.

POINT-TRUSSER, one who trussed (tied) his master's points (q.v.).

POISE, weigh, balance.

POKING-STICK, stick used for setting the plaits of ruffs.

POLITIC, politician.

POLITIC, judicious, prudent, political.

POLITICIAN, plotter, intriguer.

POLL, strip, plunder, gain by extortion.

POMANDER, ball of perfume, worn or hung about the person to prevent infection, or for foppery.

POMMADO, vaulting on a horse without the aid of stirrups.

PONTIC, sour.

POPULAR, vulgar, of the populace.

POPULOUS, numerous.

PORT, gate; print of a deer's foot.

PORT, transport.

PORTAGUE, Portuguese gold coin, worth over 3 or 4 pounds.

PORTCULLIS, "-- of coin," some old coins have a portcullis stamped on their reverse (Whalley).

PORTENT, marvel, prodigy; sinister omen.

PORTENTOUS, prophesying evil, threatening.

PORTER, references appear "to allude to Parsons, the king's porter, who was...near seven feet high" (Whalley).

POSSESS, inform, acquaint.

POST AND PAIR, a game at cards.

POSY, motto. (See Poesie).

POTCH, poach.

POULT-FOOT, club-foot.

POUNCE, claw, talon.

PRACTICE, intrigue, concerted plot.

PRACTISE, plot, conspire.

PRAGMATIC, an expert, agent.

PRAGMATIC, officious, conceited, meddling.

PRECEDENT, record of proceedings.

PRECEPT, warrant, summons.

PRECISIAN(ISM), Puritan(ism), preciseness.

PREFER, recommend.

PRESENCE, presence chamber.

PRESENT(LY), immediate(ly), without delay; at the present time; actually.

PRESS, force into service.

PREST, ready.

PRETEND, assert, allege.

PREVENT, anticipate.

PRICE, worth, excellence.

PRICK, point, dot used in the writing of Hebrew and other languages.

PRICK, prick out, mark off, select; trace, track; "-- away," make off with speed.

PRIMERO, game of cards.

PRINCOX, pert boy.

PRINT, "in --," to the letter, exactly.

PRISTINATE, former.

PRIVATE, private interests.

PRIVATE, privy, intimate.

PROCLIVE, prone to.

PRODIGIOUS, monstrous, unnatural.

PRODIGY, monster.

PRODUCED, prolonged.

PROFESS, pretend.

PROJECTION, the throwing of the "powder of projection" into the crucible to turn the melted metal into gold or silver.

PROLATE, pronounce drawlingly.

PROPER, of good appearance, handsome; own, particular.

PROPERTIES, stage necessaries.

PROPERTY, duty; tool.

PRORUMPED, burst out.

PROTEST, vow, proclaim (an affected word of that time); formally declare non-payment, etc., of bill of exchange; fig. failure of personal credit, etc.

PROVANT, soldier's allowance -- hence, of common make.

PROVIDE, foresee.

PROVIDENCE, foresight, prudence.

PUBLICATION, making a thing public of common property (N.E.D.).

PUCKFIST, puff-ball; insipid, insignificant, boasting fellow.

PUFF-WING, shoulder puff.

PUISNE, judge of inferior rank, a junior.

PULCHRITUDE, beauty.

PUMP, shoe.

PUNGENT, piercing.

PUNTO, point, hit.

PURCEPT, precept, warrant.

PURE, fine, capital, excellent.

PURELY, perfectly, utterly.

PURL, pleat or fold of a ruff.

PURSE-NET, net of which the mouth is drawn together with a string.

PURSUIVANT, state messenger who summoned the persecuted seminaries; warrant officer.

PURSY, PURSINESS, shortwinded(ness).

PUT, make a push, exert yourself (N.E.D.).

PUT OFF, excuse, shift.

PUT ON, incite, encourage; proceed with, take in hand, try.

QUACKSALVER, quack.

QUAINT, elegant, elaborated, ingenious, clever.

QUAR, quarry.

QUARRIED, seized, or fed upon, as prey.

QUEAN, hussy, jade.

QUEASY, hazardous, delicate.

QUELL, kill, destroy.

QUEST, request; inquiry.

QUESTION, decision by force of arms.

QUESTMAN, one appointed to make official inquiry.

QUIB, QUIBLIN, quibble, quip.

QUICK, the living.

QUIDDIT, quiddity, legal subtlety.

QUIRK, clever turn or trick.

QUIT, requite, repay; acquit, absolve; rid; forsake, leave.

QUITTER-BONE, disease of horses.

QUODLING, codling.

QUOIT, throw like a quoit, chuck.

QUOTE, take note, observe, write down.

RACK, neck of mutton or pork (Halliwell).

RAKE UP, cover over.

RAMP, rear, as a lion, etc.

RAPT, carry away.

RAPT, enraptured.

RASCAL, young or inferior deer.

RASH, strike with a glancing oblique blow, as a boar with its tusk.

RATSEY, GOMALIEL, a famous highwayman.

RAVEN, devour.

REACH, understand.

REAL, regal.

REBATU, ruff, turned-down collar.

RECTOR, RECTRESS, director, governor.

REDARGUE, confute.

REDUCE, bring back.

REED, rede, counsel, advice.

REEL, run riot.

REFEL, refute.

REFORMADOES, disgraced or disbanded soldiers.

REGIMENT, government.

REGRESSION, return.

REGULAR ("Tale of a Tub"), regular noun (quibble) (N.E.D.).

RELIGION, "make -- of," make a point of, scruple of.

RELISH, savour.

REMNANT, scrap of quotation.

REMORA, species of fish.

RENDER, depict, exhibit, show.

REPAIR, reinstate.

REPETITION, recital, narration.

REREMOUSE, bat.

RESIANT, resident.

RESIDENCE, sediment.

RESOLUTION, judgment, decision.

RESOLVE, inform; assure; prepare, make up one's mind; dissolve; come to a decision, be convinced; relax, set at ease.

RESPECTIVE, worthy of respect; regardful, discriminative.

RESPECTIVELY, with reverence.

RESPECTLESS, regardless.

RESPIRE, exhale; inhale.

RESPONSIBLE, correspondent.

REST, musket-rest.

REST, "set up one's --," venture one's all, one's last stake (from game of primero).

REST, arrest.

RESTIVE, RESTY, dull, inactive.

RETCHLESS(NESS), reckless(ness).

RETIRE, cause to retire.

RETRICATO, fencing term.

RETRIEVE, rediscovery of game once sprung.

RETURNS, ventures sent abroad, for the safe return of which so much money is received.

REVERBERATE, dissolve or blend by reflected heat.

REVERSE, REVERSO, back-handed thrust, etc., in fencing.

REVISE, reconsider a sentence.

RHEUM, spleen, caprice.

RIBIBE, abusive term for an old woman.

RID, destroy, do away with.

RIFLING, raffling, dicing.

RING, "cracked within the --," coins so cracked were unfit for currency.

RISSE, risen, rose.

RIVELLED, wrinkled.

ROARER, swaggerer.

ROCHET, fish of the gurnet kind.

ROCK, distaff.

RODOMONTADO, braggadocio.

ROGUE, vagrant, vagabond.

RONDEL, "a round mark in the score of a public-house" (Nares); roundel.

ROOK, sharper; fool, dupe.

ROSAKER, similar to ratsbane.

ROSA-SOLIS, a spiced spirituous liquor.

ROSES, rosettes.

ROUND, "gentlemen of the --," officers of inferior rank.

ROUND TRUNKS, trunk hose, short loose breeches reaching almost or quite to the knees.

ROUSE, carouse, bumper.

ROVER, arrow used for shooting at a random mark at uncertain distance.

ROWLY-POWLY, roly-poly.

RUDE, RUDENESS, unpolished, rough(ness), coarse(ness).

RUFFLE, flaunt, swagger.

RUG, coarse frieze.

RUG-GOWNS, gown made of rug.

RUSH, reference to rushes with which the floors were then strewn.

RUSHER, one who strewed the floor with rushes.

RUSSET, homespun cloth of neutral or reddish-brown colour.

SACK, loose, flowing gown.

SADLY, seriously, with gravity.

SAD(NESS), sober, serious(ness).

SAFFI, bailiffs.

ST. THOMAS A WATERINGS, place in Surrey where criminals were executed.

SAKER, small piece of ordnance.

SALT, leap.

SALT, lascivious.

SAMPSUCHINE, sweet marjoram.

SARABAND, a slow dance.

SATURNALS, began December 17.

SAUCINESS, presumption, insolence.

SAUCY, bold, impudent, wanton.

SAUNA (Lat.), a gesture of contempt.

SAVOUR, perceive; gratify, please; to partake of the nature.

SAY, sample.

SAY, assay, try.

SCALD, word of contempt, implying dirt and disease.

SCALLION, shalot, small onion.

SCANDERBAG, "name which the Turks (in allusion to Alexander the Great) gave to the brave Castriot, chief of Albania, with whom they had continual wars. His romantic life had just been translated" (Gifford).

SCAPE, escape.

SCARAB, beetle.

SCARTOCCIO, fold of paper, cover, cartouch, cartridge.

SCONCE, head.

SCOPE, aim.

SCOT AND LOT, tax, contribution (formerly a parish assessment).

SCOTOMY, dizziness in the head.

SCOUR, purge.

SCOURSE, deal, swap.

SCRATCHES, disease of horses.

SCROYLE, mean, rascally fellow.

SCRUPLE, doubt.

SEAL, put hand to the giving up of property or rights.

SEALED, stamped as genuine.

SEAM-RENT, ragged.

SEAMING LACES, insertion or edging.

SEAR UP, close by searing, burning.

SEARCED, sifted.

SECRETARY, able to keep a secret.

SECULAR, worldly, ordinary, commonplace.

SECURE, confident.

SEELIE, happy, blest.

SEISIN, legal term: possession.

SELLARY, lewd person.

SEMBLABLY, similarly.

SEMINARY, a Romish priest educated in a foreign seminary.

SENSELESS, insensible, without sense or feeling.

SENSIBLY, perceptibly.

SENSIVE, sensitive.

SENSUAL, pertaining to the physical or material.

SERENE, harmful dew of evening.

SERICON, red tincture.

SERVANT, lover.

SERVICES, doughty deeds of arms.

SESTERCE, Roman copper coin.

SET, stake, wager.

SET UP, drill.

SETS, deep plaits of the ruff.

SEWER, officer who served up the feast, and brought water for the hands of the guests.

SHAPE, a suit by way of disguise.

SHIFT, fraud, dodge.

SHIFTER, cheat.

SHITTLE, shuttle; "shittle-cock," shuttlecock.

SHOT, tavern reckoning.

SHOT-CLOG, one only tolerated because he paid the shot (reckoning) for the rest.

SHOT-FREE, scot-free, not having to pay.

SHOVE-GROAT, low kind of gambling amusement, perhaps somewhat of the nature of pitch and toss.

SHOT-SHARKS, drawers.

SHREWD, mischievous, malicious, curst.

SHREWDLY, keenly, in a high degree.

SHRIVE, sheriff; posts were set up before his door for proclamations, or to indicate his residence.

SHROVING, Shrovetide, season of merriment.

SIGILLA, seal, mark.

SILENCED BRETHERN, MINISTERS, those of the Church or Nonconformists who had been silenced, deprived, etc.

SILLY, simple, harmless.

SIMPLE, silly, witless; plain, true.

SIMPLES, herbs.

SINGLE, term of chase, signifying when the hunted stag is separated from the herd, or forced to break covert.

SINGLE, weak, silly.

SINGLE-MONEY, small change.

SINGULAR, unique, supreme.

SI-QUIS, bill, advertisement.

SKELDRING, getting money under false pretences; swindling.

SKILL, "it --s not," matters not.

SKINK(ER), pour, draw(er), tapster.

SKIRT, tail.

SLEEK, smooth.

SLICE, fire shovel or pan (dial.).

SLICK, sleek, smooth.

'SLID, 'SLIGHT, 'SPRECIOUS, irreverent oaths.

SLIGHT, sleight, cunning, cleverness; trick.

SLIP, counterfeit coin, bastard.

SLIPPERY, polished and shining.

SLOPS, large loose breeches.

SLOT, print of a stag's foot.

SLUR, put a slur on; cheat (by sliding a die in some way).

SMELT, gull, simpleton.

SNORLE, "perhaps snarl, as Puppy is addressed" (Cunningham).

SNOTTERIE, filth.

SNUFF, anger, resentment; "take in --," take offence at.

SNUFFERS, small open silver dishes for holding snuff, or receptacle for placing snuffers in (Halliwell).

SOCK, shoe worn by comic actors.

SOD, seethe.

SOGGY, soaked, sodden.

SOIL, "take --," said of a hunted stag when he takes to the water for safety.

SOL, sou.

SOLDADOES, soldiers.

SOLICIT, rouse, excite to action.

SOOTH, flattery, cajolery.

SOOTHE, flatter, humour.

SOPHISTICATE, adulterate.

SORT, company, party; rank, degree.

SORT, suit, fit; select.

SOUSE, ear.

SOUSED ("Devil is an Ass"), fol. read "sou't," which Dyce interprets as "a variety of the spelling of "shu'd": to "shu" is to scare a bird away." (See his "Webster," page 350).

SOWTER, cobbler.

SPAGYRICA, chemistry according to the teachings of Paracelsus.

SPAR, bar.

SPEAK, make known, proclaim.

SPECULATION, power of sight.

SPED, to have fared well, prospered.

SPEECE, species.

SPIGHT, anger, rancour.

SPINNER, spider.

SPINSTRY, lewd person.

SPITTLE, hospital, lazar-house.

SPLEEN, considered the seat of the emotions.

SPLEEN, caprice, humour, mood.

SPRUNT, spruce.

SPURGE, foam.

SPUR-RYAL, gold coin worth 15s.

SQUIRE, square, measure; "by the --," exactly.

STAGGERING, wavering, hesitating.

STAIN, disparagement, disgrace.

STALE, decoy, or cover, stalking-horse.

STALE, make cheap, common.

STALK, approach stealthily or under cover.

STALL, forestall.

STANDARD, suit.

STAPLE, market, emporium.

STARK, downright.

STARTING-HOLES, loopholes of escape.

STATE, dignity; canopied chair of state; estate.

STATUMINATE, support vines by poles or stakes; used by Pliny (Gifford).

STAY, gag.

STAY, await; detain.

STICKLER, second or umpire.

STIGMATISE, mark, brand.

STILL, continual(ly), constant(ly).

STINKARD, stinking fellow.

STINT, stop.

STIPTIC, astringent.

STOCCATA, thrust in fencing.

STOCK-FISH, salted and dried fish.

STOMACH, pride, valour.

STOMACH, resent.

STOOP, swoop down as a hawk.

STOP, fill, stuff.

STOPPLE, stopper.

STOTE, stoat, weasel.

STOUP, stoop, swoop=bow.

STRAIGHT, straightway.

STRAMAZOUN (Ital. stramazzone), a down blow, as opposed to the thrust.

STRANGE, like a stranger, unfamiliar.

STRANGENESS, distance of behaviour.

STREIGHTS, OR BERMUDAS, labyrinth of alleys and courts in the Strand.

STRIGONIUM, Grau in Hungary, taken from the Turks in 1597.

STRIKE, balance (accounts).

STRINGHALT, disease of horses.

STROKER, smoother, flatterer.

STROOK, p.p. of "strike".

STRUMMEL-PATCHED, strummel is glossed in dialect dicts. as "a long, loose and dishevelled head of hair".

STUDIES, studious efforts.

STYLE, title; pointed instrument used for writing on wax tablets.

SUBTLE, fine, delicate, thin; smooth, soft.

SUBTLETY (SUBTILITY), subtle device.

SUBURB, connected with loose living.

SUCCUBAE, demons in form of women.

SUCK, extract money from.

SUFFERANCE, suffering.

SUMMED, term of falconry: with full-grown plumage.

SUPER-NEGULUM, topers turned the cup bottom up when it was empty.

SUPERSTITIOUS, over-scrupulous.

SUPPLE, to make pliant.

SURBATE, make sore with walking.

SURCEASE, cease.

SUR-REVERENCE, save your reverence.

SURVISE, peruse.

SUSCITABILITY, excitability.

SUSPECT, suspicion.

SUSPEND, suspect.

SUSPENDED, held over for the present.

SUTLER, victualler.

SWAD, clown, boor.

SWATH BANDS, swaddling clothes.

SWINGE, beat.

TABERD, emblazoned mantle or tunic worn by knights and heralds.

TABLE(S), "pair of --," tablets, note-book.

TABOR, small drum.

TABRET, tabor.

TAFFETA, silk; "tuft-taffeta," a more costly silken fabric.

TAINT, "-- a staff," break a lance at tilting in an unscientific or dishonourable manner.

TAKE IN, capture, subdue.

TAKE ME WITH YOU, let me understand you.

TAKE UP, obtain on credit, borrow.

TALENT, sum or weight of Greek currency.

TALL, stout, brave.

TANKARD-BEARERS, men employed to fetch water from the conduits.

TARLETON, celebrated comedian and jester.

TARTAROUS, like a Tartar.

TAVERN-TOKEN, "to swallow a --," get drunk.

TELL, count.

TELL-TROTH, truth-teller.

TEMPER, modify, soften.

TENDER, show regard, care for, cherish; manifest.

TENT, "take --," take heed.

TERSE, swept and polished.

TERTIA, "that portion of an army levied out of one particular district or division of a country" (Gifford).

TESTON, tester, coin worth 6d.

THIRDBOROUGH, constable.

THREAD, quality.

THREAVES, droves.

THREE-FARTHINGS, piece of silver current under Elizabeth.

THREE-PILED, of finest quality, exaggerated.

THRIFTILY, carefully.

THRUMS, ends of the weaver's warp; coarse yarn made from.

THUMB-RING, familiar spirits were supposed capable of being carried about in various ornaments or parts of dress.

TIBICINE, player on the tibia, or pipe.

TICK-TACK, game similar to backgammon.

TIGHTLY, promptly.

TIM, (?) expressive of a climax of nonentity.

TIMELESS, untimely, unseasonable.

TINCTURE, an essential or spiritual principle supposed by alchemists to be transfusible into material things; an imparted characteristic or tendency.

TINK, tinkle.

TIPPET, "turn --," change behaviour or way of life.

TIPSTAFF, staff tipped with metal.

TIRE, head-dress.

TIRE, feed ravenously, like a bird of prey.

TITILLATION, that which tickles the senses, as a perfume.

TOD, fox.

TOILED, worn out, harassed.

TOKEN, piece of base metal used in place of very small coin, when this was scarce.

TONNELS, nostrils.

TOP, "parish --," large top kept in villages for amusement and exercise in frosty weather when people were out of work.

TOTER, tooter, player on a wind instrument.

TOUSE, pull, rend.

TOWARD, docile, apt; on the way to; as regards; present, at hand.

TOY, whim; trick; term of contempt.

TRACT, attraction.

TRAIN, allure, entice.

TRANSITORY, transmittable.

TRANSLATE, transform.

TRAY-TRIP, game at dice (success depended on throwing a three) (Nares).

TREACHOUR (TRECHER), traitor.

TREEN, wooden.

TRENCHER, serving-man who carved or served food.

TRENDLE-TAIL, trundle-tail, curly-tailed.

TRICK (TRICKING), term of heraldry: to draw outline of coat of arms, etc., without blazoning.

TRIG, a spruce, dandified man.

TRILL, trickle.

TRILLIBUB, tripe, any worthless, trifling thing.

TRIPOLY, "come from --," able to perform feats of agility, a "jest nominal," depending on the first part of the word (Gifford).

TRITE, worn, shabby.

TRIVIA, three-faced goddess (Hecate).

TROJAN, familiar term for an equal or inferior; thief.

TROLL, sing loudly.

TROMP, trump, deceive.

TROPE, figure of speech.

TROW, think, believe, wonder.

TROWLE, troll.

TROWSES, breeches, drawers.

TRUCHMAN, interpreter.

TRUNDLE, JOHN, well-known printer.

TRUNDLE, roll, go rolling along.

TRUNDLING CHEATS, term among gipsies and beggars for

carts or coaches (Gifford).

TRUNK, speaking-tube.

TRUSS, tie the tagged laces that fastened the breeches to the doublet.

TUBICINE, trumpeter.

TUCKET (Ital. toccato), introductory flourish on the trumpet.

TUITION, guardianship.

TUMBLER, a particular kind of dog so called from the mode of his hunting.

TUMBREL-SLOP, loose, baggy breeches.

TURD, excrement.

TUSK, gnash the teeth (Century Dict.).

TWIRE, peep, twinkle.

TWOPENNY ROOM, gallery.

TYRING-HOUSE, attiring-room.

ULENSPIEGEL. See Howleglass.

UMBRATILE, like or pertaining to a shadow.

UMBRE, brown dye.

UNBATED, unabated.

UNBORED, (?) excessively bored.

UNCARNATE, not fleshly, or of flesh.

UNCOUTH, strange, unusual.

UNDERTAKER, "one who undertook by his influence in the House of Commons to carry things agreeably to his Majesty's wishes" (Whalley); one who becomes surety for.

UNEQUAL, unjust.

UNEXCEPTED, no objection taken at.

UNFEARED, unaffrighted.

UNHAPPILY, unfortunately.

UNICORN'S HORN, supposed antidote to poison.

UNKIND(LY), unnatural(ly).

UNMANNED, untamed (term in falconry).

UNQUIT, undischarged.

UNREADY, undressed.

UNRUDE, rude to an extreme.

UNSEASONED, unseasonable, unripe.

UNSEELED, a hawk's eyes were "seeled" by sewing the eyelids together with fine thread.

UNTIMELY, unseasonably.

UNVALUABLE, invaluable.

UPBRAID, make a matter of reproach.

UPSEE, heavy kind of Dutch beer (Halliwell); "-- Dutch," in the Dutch fashion.

UPTAILS ALL, refrain of a popular song.

URGE, allege as accomplice, instigator.

URSHIN, URCHIN, hedgehog.

USE, interest on money; part of sermon dealing with the practical application of doctrine.

USE, be in the habit of, accustomed to; put out to interest.

USQUEBAUGH, whisky.

USURE, usury.

UTTER, put in circulation, make to pass current; put forth for sale.

VAIL, bow, do homage.

VAILS, tips, gratuities.

VALL. See Vail.

VALLIES (Fr. valise), portmanteau, bag.

VAPOUR(S) (n. and v.), used affectedly, like "humour," in many senses, often very vaguely and freely ridiculed by Jonson; humour, disposition, whims, brag(ging), hector(ing), etc.

VARLET, bailiff, or serjeant-at-mace.

VAUT, vault.

VEER (naut.), pay out.

VEGETAL, vegetable; person full of life and vigour.

VELLUTE, velvet.

VELVET CUSTARD. Cf. "Taming of the Shrew," iv. 3, 82, "custard coffin," coffin being the raised crust over a pie.

VENT, vend, sell; give outlet to; scent, snuff up.

VENUE, bout (fencing term).

VERDUGO (Span.), hangman, executioner.

VERGE, "in the --," within a certain distance of the court.

VEX, agitate, torment.

VICE, the buffoon of old moralities; some kind of machinery for moving a puppet (Gifford).

VIE AND REVIE, to hazard a certain sum, and to cover it with a larger one.

VINCENT AGAINST YORK, two heralds-at-arms.

VINDICATE, avenge.

VIRGE, wand, rod.

VIRGINAL, old form of piano.

VIRTUE, valour.

VIVELY, in lifelike manner, livelily.

VIZARD, mask.

VOGUE, rumour, gossip.

VOICE, vote.

VOID, leave, quit.

VOLARY, cage, aviary.

VOLLEY, "at --," "o' the volee," at random (from a term of tennis).

VORLOFFE, furlough.

WADLOE, keeper of the Devil Tavern, where Jonson and his friends met in the 'Apollo' room (Whalley).

WAIGHTS, waits, night musicians, "band of musical watchmen" (Webster), or old form of "hautboys".

WANNION, "vengeance," "plague" (Nares).

WARD, a famous pirate.

WARD, guard in fencing.

WATCHET, pale, sky blue.

WEAL, welfare.

WEED, garment.

WEFT, waif.

WEIGHTS, "to the gold --," to every minute particular.

WELKIN, sky.

WELL-SPOKEN, of fair speech.

WELL-TORNED, turned and polished, as on a wheel.

WELT, hem, border of fur.

WHER, whether.

WHETSTONE, GEORGE, an author who lived 1544(?) to 1587(?).

WHIFF, a smoke, or drink; "taking the --," inhaling the tobacco smoke or some such accomplishment.

WHIGH-HIES, neighings, whinnyings.

WHIMSY, whim, "humour".

WHINILING, (?) whining, weakly.

WHIT, (?) a mere jot.

WHITEMEAT, food made of milk or eggs.

WICKED, bad, clumsy.

WICKER, pliant, agile.

WILDING, esp. fruit of wild apple or crab tree (Webster).

WINE, "I have the -- for you," Prov.: I have the perquisites (of the office) which you are to share (Cunningham).

WINNY, "same as old word "wonne," to stay, etc." (Whalley).

WISE-WOMAN, fortune-teller.

WISH, recommend.

WISS (WUSSE), "I --," certainly, of a truth.

WITHOUT, beyond.

WITTY, cunning, ingenious, clever.

WOOD, collection, lot.

WOODCOCK, term of contempt.

WOOLSACK ("-- pies"), name of tavern.

WORT, unfermented beer.

WOUNDY, great, extreme.

WREAK, revenge.

WROUGHT, wrought upon.

WUSSE, interjection. (See Wiss).

YEANLING, lamb, kid.

ZANY, an inferior clown, who attended upon the chief fool and mimicked his tricks.

www.bookjungle.com *email: sales@bookjungle.com fax: 630-214-0564 mail: Book Jungle PO Box 2226 Champaign, IL 61825*

The Codes Of Hammurabi And Moses
W. W. Davies

QTY

The discovery of the Hammurabi Code is one of the greatest achievements of archaeology, and is of paramount interest, not only to the student of the Bible, but also to all those interested in ancient history...

Religion   **ISBN:** *1-59462-338-4*   **Pages:132**
MSRP $12.95

The Theory of Moral Sentiments
Adam Smith

QTY

This work from 1749. contains original theories of conscience amd moral judgment and it is the foundation for systemof morals.

Philosophy   **ISBN:** *1-59462-777-0*   **Pages:536**
MSRP $19.95

Jessica's First Prayer
Hesba Stretton

QTY

In a screened and secluded corner of one of the many railway-bridges which span the streets of London there could be seen a few years ago, from five o'clock every morning until half past eight, a tidily set-out coffee-stall, consisting of a trestle and board, upon which stood two large tin cans, with a small fire of charcoal burning under each so as to keep the coffee boiling during the early hours of the morning when the work-people were thronging into the city on their way to their daily toil...

Childrens   **ISBN:** *1-59462-373-2*   **Pages:84**
MSRP $9.95

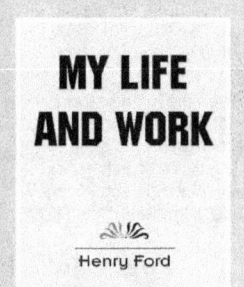

My Life and Work
Henry Ford

QTY

Henry Ford revolutionized the world with his implementation of mass production for the Model T automobile. Gain valuable business insight into his life and work with his own auto-biography... "We have only started on our development of our country we have not as yet, with all our talk of wonderful progress, done more than scratch the surface. The progress has been wonderful enough but..."

Biographies/   **ISBN:** *1-59462-198-5*   **Pages:300**
MSRP $21.95

www.bookjungle.com *email: sales@bookjungle.com fax: 630-214-0564 mail: Book Jungle PO Box 2226 Champaign, IL 61825*

The Art of Cross-Examination
Francis Wellman

QTY

I presume it is the experience of every author, after his first book is published upon an important subject, to be almost overwhelmed with a wealth of ideas and illustrations which could readily have been included in his book, and which to his own mind, at least, seem to make a second edition inevitable. Such certainly was the case with me; and when the first edition had reached its sixth impression in five months, I rejoiced to learn that it seemed to my publishers that the book had met with a sufficiently favorable reception to justify a second and considerably enlarged edition. ..

Reference   ISBN: *1-59462-647-2*

Pages:412
MSRP *$19.95*

On the Duty of Civil Disobedience
Henry David Thoreau

QTY

Thoreau wrote his famous essay, On the Duty of Civil Disobedience, as a protest against an unjust but popular war and the immoral but popular institution of slave-owning. He did more than write—he declined to pay his taxes, and was hauled off to gaol in consequence. Who can say how much this refusal of his hastened the end of the war and of slavery ?

Law   ISBN: *1-59462-747-9*

Pages:48
MSRP *$7.45*

Dream Psychology Psychoanalysis for Beginners
Sigmund Freud

QTY

Sigmund Freud, born Sigismund Schlomo Freud (May 6, 1856 - September 23, 1939), was a Jewish-Austrian neurologist and psychiatrist who co-founded the psychoanalytic school of psychology. Freud is best known for his theories of the unconscious mind, especially involving the mechanism of repression; his redefinition of sexual desire as mobile and directed towards a wide variety of objects; and his therapeutic techniques, especially his understanding of transference in the therapeutic relationship and the presumed value of dreams as sources of insight into unconscious desires.

Psychology   ISBN: *1-59462-905-6*

Pages:196
MSRP *$15.45*

The Miracle of Right Thought
Orison Swett Marden

QTY

Believe with all of your heart that you will do what you were made to do. When the mind has once formed the habit of holding cheerful, happy, prosperous pictures, it will not be easy to form the opposite habit. It does not matter how improbable or how far away this realization may see, or how dark the prospects may be, if we visualize them as best we can, as vividly as possible, hold tenaciously to them and vigorously struggle to attain them, they will gradually become actualized, realized in the life. But a desire, a longing without endeavor, a yearning abandoned or held indifferently will vanish without realization.

Self Help   ISBN: *1-59462-644-8*

Pages:360
MSRP *$25.45*

www.bookjungle.com email: sales@bookjungle.com fax: 630-214-0564 mail: Book Jungle PO Box 2226 Champaign, IL 61825

QTY

	Title	ISBN	Price
☐	**The Rosicrucian Cosmo-Conception Mystic Christianity** by *Max Heindel*	ISBN: 1-59462-188-8	$38.95
	The Rosicrucian Cosmo-conception is not dogmatic, neither does it appeal to any other authority than the reason of the student. It is: not controversial, but is: sent forth in the, hope that it may help to clear...	New Age/Religion Pages 646	
☐	**Abandonment To Divine Providence** by *Jean-Pierre de Caussade*	ISBN: 1-59462-228-0	$25.95
	"The Rev. Jean Pierre de Caussade was one of the most remarkable spiritual writers of the Society of Jesus in France in the 18th Century. His death took place at Toulouse in 1751. His works have gone through many editions and have been republished...	Inspirational/Religion Pages 400	
☐	**Mental Chemistry** by *Charles Haanel*	ISBN: 1-59462-192-6	$23.95
	Mental Chemistry allows the change of material conditions by combining and appropriately utilizing the power of the mind. Much like applied chemistry creates something new and unique out of careful combinations of chemicals the mastery of mental chemistry...	New Age Pages 354	
☐	**The Letters of Robert Browning and Elizabeth Barret Barrett 1845-1846 vol II** by *Robert Browning* and *Elizabeth Barrett*	ISBN: 1-59462-193-4	$35.95
		Biographies Pages 596	
☐	**Gleanings In Genesis (volume I)** by *Arthur W. Pink*	ISBN: 1-59462-130-6	$27.45
	Appropriately has Genesis been termed "the seed plot of the Bible" for in it we have, in germ form, almost all of the great doctrines which are afterwards fully developed in the books of Scripture which follow...	Religion/Inspirational Pages 420	
☐	**The Master Key** by *L. W. de Laurence*	ISBN: 1-59462-001-6	$30.95
	In no branch of human knowledge has there been a more lively increase of the spirit of research during the past few years than in the study of Psychology, Concentration and Mental Discipline. The requests for authentic lessons in Thought Control, Mental Discipline and...	New Age/Business Pages 422	
☐	**The Lesser Key Of Solomon Goetia** by *L. W. de Laurence*	ISBN: 1-59462-092-X	$9.95
	This translation of the first book of the "Lernegton" which is now for the first time made accessible to students of Talismanic Magic was done, after careful collation and edition, from numerous Ancient Manuscripts in Hebrew, Latin, and French...	New Age/Occult Pages 92	
☐	**Rubaiyat Of Omar Khayyam** by *Edward Fitzgerald*	ISBN: 1-59462-332-5	$13.95
	Edward Fitzgerald, whom the world has already learned, in spite of his own efforts to remain within the shadow of anonymity, to look upon as one of the rarest poets of the century, was born at Bredfield, in Suffolk, on the 31st of March, 1809. He was the third son of John Purcell...	Music Pages 172	
☐	**Ancient Law** by *Henry Maine*	ISBN: 1-59462-128-4	$29.95
	The chief object of the following pages is to indicate some of the earliest ideas of mankind, as they are reflected in Ancient Law, and to point out the relation of those ideas to modern thought.	Religion/History Pages 452	
☐	**Far-Away Stories** by *William J. Locke*	ISBN: 1-59462-129-2	$19.45
	"Good wine needs no bush, but a collection of mixed vintages does. And this book is just such a collection. Some of the stories I do not want to remain buried for ever in the museum files of dead magazine-numbers an author's not unpardonable vanity..."	Fiction Pages 272	
☐	**Life of David Crockett** by *David Crockett*	ISBN: 1-59462-250-7	$27.45
	"Colonel David Crockett was one of the most remarkable men of the times in which he lived. Born in humble life, but gifted with a strong will, an indomitable courage, and unremitting perseverance...	Biographies/New Age Pages 424	
☐	**Lip-Reading** by *Edward Nitchie*	ISBN: 1-59462-206-X	$25.95
	Edward B. Nitchie, founder of the New York School for the Hard of Hearing, now the Nitchie School of Lip-Reading, Inc, wrote "LIP-READING Principles and Practice". The development and perfecting of this meritorious work on lip-reading was an undertaking...	How-to Pages 400	
☐	**A Handbook of Suggestive Therapeutics, Applied Hypnotism, Psychic Science** by *Henry Munro*	ISBN: 1-59462-214-0	$24.95
		Health/New Age/Health/Self-help Pages 376	
☐	**A Doll's House: and Two Other Plays** by *Henrik Ibsen*	ISBN: 1-59462-112-8	$19.95
	Henrik Ibsen created this classic when in revolutionary 1848 Rome. Introducing some striking concepts in playwriting for the realist genre, this play has been studied the world over.	Fiction/Classics/Plays 308	
☐	**The Light of Asia** by *sir Edwin Arnold*	ISBN: 1-59462-204-3	$13.95
	In this poetic masterpiece, Edwin Arnold describes the life and teachings of Buddha. The man who was to become known as Buddha to the world was born as Prince Gautama of India but he rejected the worldly riches and abandoned the reigns of power when...	Religion/History/Biographies Pages 170	
☐	**The Complete Works of Guy de Maupassant** by *Guy de Maupassant*	ISBN: 1-59462-157-8	$16.95
	"For days and days, nights and nights, I had dreamed of that first kiss which was to consecrate our engagement, and I knew not on what spot I should put my lips..."	Fiction/Classics Pages 240	
☐	**The Art of Cross-Examination** by *Francis L. Wellman*	ISBN: 1-59462-309-0	$26.95
	Written by a renowned trial lawyer, Wellman imparts his experience and uses case studies to explain how to use psychology to extract desired information through questioning.	How-to/Science/Reference Pages 408	
☐	**Answered or Unanswered?** by *Louisa Vaughan*	ISBN: 1-59462-248-5	$10.95
	Miracles of Faith in China	Religion Pages 112	
☐	**The Edinburgh Lectures on Mental Science (1909)** by *Thomas*	ISBN: 1-59462-008-3	$11.95
	This book contains the substance of a course of lectures recently given by the writer in the Queen Street Hall, Edinburgh. Its purpose is to indicate the Natural Principles governing the relation between Mental Action and Material Conditions...	New Age/Psychology Pages 148	
☐	**Ayesha** by *H. Rider Haggard*	ISBN: 1-59462-301-5	$24.95
	Verily and indeed it is the unexpected that happens! Probably if there was one person upon the earth from whom the Editor of this, and of a certain previous history, did not expect to hear again...	Classics Pages 380	
☐	**Ayala's Angel** by *Anthony Trollope*	ISBN: 1-59462-352-X	$29.95
	The two girls were both pretty, but Lucy who was twenty-one who supposed to be simple and comparatively unattractive, whereas Ayala was credited, as her Bombwhat romantic name might show, with poetic charm and a taste for romance. Ayala when her father died was nineteen...	Fiction Pages 484	
☐	**The American Commonwealth** by *James Bryce*	ISBN: 1-59462-286-8	$34.45
	An interpretation of American democratic political theory. It examines political mechanics and society from the perspective of Scotsman James Bryce	Politics Pages 572	
☐	**Stories of the Pilgrims** by *Margaret P. Pumphrey*	ISBN: 1-59462-116-0	$17.95
	This book explores pilgrims religious oppression in England as well as their escape to Holland and eventual crossing to America on the Mayflower, and their early days in New England...	History Pages 268	

www.bookjungle.com *email: sales@bookjungle.com fax: 630-214-0564 mail: Book Jungle PO Box 2226 Champaign, IL 61825*

QTY

The Fasting Cure by *Sinclair Upton* ISBN: *1-59462-222-1* **$13.95**
In the Cosmopolitan Magazine for May, 1910, and in the Contemporary Review (London) for April, 1910, I published an article dealing with my experiences in fasting. I have written a great many magazine articles, but never one which attracted so much attention... New Age/Self Help/Health Pages 164

Hebrew Astrology by *Sepharial* ISBN: *1-59462-308-2* **$13.45**
In these days of advanced thinking it is a matter of common observation that we have left many of the old landmarks behind and that we are now pressing forward to greater heights and to a wider horizon than that which represented the mind-content of our progenitors... Astrology Pages 144

Thought Vibration or The Law of Attraction in the Thought World ISBN: *1-59462-127-6* **$12.95**
by *William Walker Atkinson* Psychology/Religion Pages 144

Optimism by *Helen Keller* ISBN: *1-59462-108-X* **$15.95**
Helen Keller was blind, deaf, and mute since 19 months old, yet famously learned how to overcome these handicaps, communicate with the world, and spread her lectures promoting optimism. An inspiring read for everyone... Biographies/Inspirational Pages 84

Sara Crewe by *Frances Burnett* ISBN: *1-59462-360-0* **$9.45**
In the first place, Miss Minchin lived in London. Her home was a large, dull, tall one, in a large, dull square, where all the houses were alike, and all the sparrows were alike, and where all the door-knockers made the same heavy sound... Childrens/Classic Pages 88

The Autobiography of Benjamin Franklin by *Benjamin Franklin* ISBN: *1-59462-135-7* **$24.95**
The Autobiography of Benjamin Franklin has probably been more extensively read than any other American historical work, and no other book of its kind has had such ups and downs of fortune. Franklin lived for many years in England, where he was agent... Biographies/History Pages 332

Name	
Email	
Telephone	
Address	
City, State ZIP	

☐ Credit Card ☐ Check / Money Order

Credit Card Number	
Expiration Date	
Signature	

Please Mail to: Book Jungle
PO Box 2226
Champaign, IL 61825
or Fax to: 630-214-0564

ORDERING INFORMATION
web: *www.bookjungle.com*
email: *sales@bookjungle.com*
fax: *630-214-0564*
mail: *Book Jungle PO Box 2226 Champaign, IL 61825*
or PayPal *to sales@bookjungle.com*

Please contact us for bulk discounts

DIRECT-ORDER TERMS

20% Discount if You Order Two or More Books
Free Domestic Shipping!
Accepted: Master Card, Visa, Discover, American Express

www.ingramcontent.com/pod-product-compliance
Lightning Source LLC
Chambersburg PA
CBHW082108230426
43671CB00015B/2640